Rush-Hour Recipes

Jean Paré

companyscoming.com
visit our web-site

Front Cover

1. Mushroom Focaccia, page 22
2. Tex-Mex Salad, page 47
3. Red Tuna Sauce, page 96
4. Sweet Chocolate Pie, page 129

Back Cover

1. Coconut Fruit Smoothie, page 12
2. Blueberry Muffins, page 33
3. Breakfast Quesadillas, page 10
4. Taco Loaf, page 28

Rush-Hour Recipes

Copyright © Company's Coming Publishing Limited

All rights reserved worldwide. No part of this book may be reproduced in any form by any means without written permission in advance from the publisher. Brief portions of this book may be reproduced for review purposes, provided credit is given to the source. Reviewers are invited to contact the publisher for additional information.

Third Printing September 2002

National Library of Canada Cataloguing in Publication

Paré, Jean

      Rush-hour recipes / Jean Paré.

(Original series)
Includes index.
ISBN 1-895455-94-4

      1. Quick and easy cookery. I. Title. II. Series: Paré, Jean. Original series.

TX833.5.P368 2002   641.5'55   C2002-901790-4

Published by
COMPANY'S COMING PUBLISHING LIMITED
2311 - 96 Street
Edmonton, Alberta, Canada T6N 1G3
Tel: (780) 450-6223   Fax: (780) 450-1857
www.companyscoming.com

Company's Coming is a registered trademark owned by Company's Coming Publishing Limited

Printed in Canada

Visit us on-line

companyscoming.com

Who We Are | Browse Cookbooks | Cooking Tonight? | Home

everyday ingredients

feature recipes

feature recipes — Cooking tonight? Check out this month's **feature recipes**—absolutely FREE!

tips and tricks — Looking for some great kitchen helpers? **tips and tricks** are here to save the day!

reader circle — In search of answers to cooking or household questions? Do you have answers you'd like to share? Join the fun with **reader circle**, our on-line question and answer bulletin board. Great for swapping recipes too!

cooking links — Other interesting and informative web-sites are just a click away with **cooking links.**

cookbook search — Find cookbooks by title, description or food category using **cookbook search**.

contact us — We want to hear from you—**contact us** lets you offer suggestions for upcoming titles, or share your favourite recipes.

Company's Coming

Canada's **most popular cookbooks!**

Company's Coming Cookbook Series

Original Series

- Softcover, 160 pages
- 6" x 9" (15 cm x 23 cm) format
- Lay-flat binding
- Full colour photos
- Nutrition information

Greatest Hits Series

- Softcover, 106 & 124 pages
- 8" x 9 9/16" (20 cm x 24 cm) format
- Paperback binding
- Full colour photos
- Nutrition information

Lifestyle Series

- Softcover, 160 pages
- 8" x 10" (20 cm x 25 cm) format
- Paperback & spiral binding
- Full colour photos
- Nutrition information

Special Occasion Series

- Hardcover & softcover, 192 pages
- 8 1/2" x 11" (22 cm x 28 cm) format
- Durable sewn binding
- Full colour throughout
- Nutrition information

See page 157
for a complete listing
of **all** cookbooks
or visit
companyscoming.com

Table of Contents

The Company's Coming Story

Jean Paré grew up understanding that the combination of family, friends and home cooking is the essence of a good life. From her mother she learned to appreciate good cooking, while her father praised even her earliest attempts. When she left home she took with her many acquired family recipes, a love of cooking and an intriguing desire to read recipe books like novels!

"never share a recipe you wouldn't use yourself"

In 1963, when her four children had all reached school age, Jean volunteered to cater the 50th anniversaryof the Vermilion School of Agriculture, now Lakeland College. Working out of her home, Jean prepared a dinner for over 1000 people which launched a flourishing catering operation that continued for over eighteen years. During that time she was provided with countless opportunities to test new ideas with immediate feedback—resulting in empty plates and contented customers! Whether preparing cocktail sandwiches for a house party or serving a hot meal for 1500 people, Jean Paré earned a reputation for good food, courteous service and reasonable prices.

"Why don't you write a cookbook?" Time and again, as requests for her recipes mounted, Jean was asked that question. Jean's response was to team up with her son, Grant Lovig, in the fall of 1980 to form Company's Coming Publishing Limited. April 14, 1981, marked the debut of "150 DELICIOUS SQUARES", the first Company's Coming cookbook in what soon would become Canada's most popular cookbook series.

Jean Paré's operation has grown steadily from the early days of working out of a spare bedroom in her home. Full-time staff includes marketing personnel located in major cities across Canada. Home Office is based in Edmonton, Alberta in a modern building constructed specially for the company.

Today the company distributes throughout Canada and the United States in addition to numerous overseas markets, all under the guidance of Jean's daughter, Gail Lovig. Best-sellers many times over in English, Company's Coming cookbooks have also been published in French and Spanish. Familiar and trusted in home kitchens around the world, Company's Coming cookbooks are offered in a variety of formats, including the original softcover series.

Jean Paré's approach to cooking has always called for quick and easy recipes using everyday ingredients. Even when travelling, she is constantly on the lookout for new ideas to share with her readers. At home, she can usually be found researching and writing recipes, or working in the company's test kitchen. Jean continues to gain new supporters by adhering to what she calls "the golden rule of cooking": never share a recipe you wouldn't use yourself. It's an approach that works— *millions of times over!*

Foreword

The real rush hour starts when you get home at the end of the day. Your meeting ran late, the kids are hungry, and everyone has to be somewhere in an hour. How are you going to get a hot, tasty meal on the table in such a short time? It's easy! *Rush-Hour Recipes* is the answer!

I remember many "rush hours" when my children were young. They had busy schedules with commitments most evenings. There was little time for meal planning and preparation. They are now cooking for their own families and face the same challenges.

Rush-Hour Recipes is full of easy-to-prepare recipes and time-saving tips. As well, the approximate number of minutes "from start to finish" is shown in the stopwatch icon beside each recipe title. These times include chopping, measuring, preparing and cooking (or baking), but do not account for defrosting. All of these recipes (with the exception of our special *Plan-Ahead Dishes* section) can be on your table in 45 minutes or less! And most call for fewer than 12 ingredients, many of which are probably in your kitchen pantry already. Simply choose a recipe and, with just a few simple steps, put a great meal on the table.

I've also discovered that keeping pre-packaged goods on hand can save a lot of time. Sauces, dressings, canned soups, frozen foods, and pre-cut meats and vegetables are all available in convenience packaging. Because many of these products are already flavoured or chopped, they can be added directly to the recipe!

There are also numerous kitchen appliances that save time and effort. A microwave or pressure cooker saves cooking time, a blender or food processor saves chopping time and a barbecue means no baking pans to scrub. Having several pots and pans and at least two frying pans can also help to

reduce overall preparation or cooking time by allowing you to do two similar steps at the same time.

For occasions when you have time to plan for the next day's meal, there's a section of *Plan-Ahead Dishes* where some, or all, of the preparation can be done the night before or in the morning. Or let your slow cooker take care of dinner while you're away for the day. And don't forget the advantage of leftovers. You can create almost-new meals even faster the next day.

So make your "rush hour" less hectic. Feed your family in no time at all with *Rush-Hour Recipes*.

Jean Paré

Each recipe has been analyzed using the most up-to-date version of the Canadian Nutrient File from Health Canada, which is based on the United States Department of Agriculture (USDA) Nutrient Data Base. If more that one ingredient is listed (such as "hard margarine or butter"), then the first ingredient is used in the analysis. Where an ingredient reads "sprinkle", "optional", or "for garnish", it is not included as part of the nutrition information.

Margaret Ng, B.Sc. (Hon), M.A.
Registered Dietitian

One-Dish Eggs

Good balance of egg and potato. While the bacon is frying, dice the peppers.
Make for breakfast, or for lunch with a fresh salad.

Bacon slices, diced	6	6
Chopped onion	1/3 cup	75 mL
Frozen hash brown potatoes	1 1/2 cups	375 mL
Finely diced green pepper	1 tbsp.	15 mL
Finely diced red pepper	1 tbsp.	15 mL
Dill weed	1/2 tsp.	2 mL
Salt	1/8 tsp.	0.5 mL
Pepper	1/8 tsp.	0.5 mL
Large eggs	6	6
Milk	1/2 cup	125 mL

Fresh dill sprigs, for garnish

Fry bacon and onion in large frying pan on medium-high for about 8 minutes, stirring frequently, until onion is golden. Transfer to small bowl using slotted spoon. Drain fat, reserving 1 tbsp. (15 mL) in frying pan.

Add hash brown potatoes, both peppers, dill weed, salt and pepper to same frying pan. Cook for 10 minutes, stirring occasionally. Add bacon mixture. Stir.

Beat eggs and milk together in small bowl. Add to bacon mixture. Cook for 1 to 2 minutes, stirring constantly using wide spatula, until eggs are cooked but not dry.

Garnish with dill sprigs. Makes 3 1/2 cups (875 mL). Serves 4.

1 serving: 283 Calories; 16.3 g Total Fat; 358 mg Sodium; 15 g Protein; 19 g Carbohydrate; 2 g Dietary Fibre

Pictured on page 35.

 To make tortillas easier to fold, sprinkle individual tortillas with water. Microwave, one at a time, on high (100%) for 20 seconds.

Breakfast

Scrambled Egg Sandwich

Similar to a Denver or Western sandwich. Great for a quick breakfast or lunch.

Finely chopped green onion	1 tbsp.	15 mL
Finely chopped green pepper	1 tbsp.	15 mL
Hard margarine (or butter)	1 tsp.	5 mL
Large egg	1	1
Water	2 tbsp.	30 mL
Finely chopped smoked ham	2 tbsp.	30 mL
Salt	1/16 tsp.	0.5 mL
Pepper	1/16 tsp.	0.5 mL
Hot pepper sauce, to taste (optional)		
Hard margarine (or butter), softened	1 – 2 tsp.	5 – 10 mL
White bread slices (toasted, optional)	2	2

Sauté green onion and green pepper in first amount of margarine in small frying pan until soft.

While green onion and green pepper are sautéing, beat egg and water with fork in small bowl. Add ham, salt, pepper and hot pepper sauce. Stir. Add to softened green onion mixture. Heat and stir on medium until egg is set but not dry.

Divide and spread second amount of margarine on 1 side of both bread slices. Spoon egg mixture onto 1 slice. Place remaining bread slice on top. Makes 1 sandwich.

1 sandwich: 314 Calories; 16.2 g Total Fat; 840 mg Sodium; 15 g Protein; 27 g Carbohydrate; 1 g Dietary Fibre

Variation: Omit ham. Use same amount cooked crisp and crumbled bacon.

Paré Pointer

Don't trust pigs with secrets. They are the worst squealers you can find.

Quick Sauced Eggs

Very good mushroom flavour with a bit of pimiento in every bite.

Large eggs	6	6
Boiling water		
Can of condensed cream of mushroom soup	10 oz.	284 mL
Grated medium (or sharp) Cheddar cheese	1/3 cup	75 mL
Chopped pimiento	1 tbsp.	15 mL
White (or whole wheat) bread slices	4	4
Thinly sliced green onion, for garnish	2 tbsp.	30 mL

Cook eggs in their shell in boiling water in large saucepan for 10 minutes. Drain. Rinse under cold running water. Peel. Cut into quarters lengthwise.

While eggs are cooking, combine soup, cheese and pimiento in medium saucepan. Heat and stir on medium-low until hot and cheese is melted. Add quartered eggs. Stir. Cook until heated through.

While mixture is heating, toast bread slices. Spoon egg mixture over toast. Garnish with green onion. Serves 4.

1 serving: 313 Calories; 17.6 g Total Fat; 935 mg Sodium; 16 g Protein; 22 g Carbohydrate; 1 g Dietary Fibre

Breakfast Quesadillas

Quesadillas make the perfect "to-go" food—breakfast, lunch or supper. These have a wonderful sausage flavour.

Package of frozen sausage meat, thawed	13 oz.	375 g
Frozen hash brown potatoes	1 cup	250 mL
Grated Monterey Jack (or Monterey Jack With Jalapeño) cheese	1 1/2 cups	375 mL
Sliced green onion	1/3 cup	75 mL
Large flour (or spinach) tortillas (about 10 inches, 25 cm), see Tip, page 8	6	6

(continued on next page)

Scramble-fry sausage meat in large frying pan until no longer pink. Drain.

Add hash brown potatoes. Cook until well browned.

Layer 1/3 cup (75 mL) sausage mixture, 1/4 cup (60 mL) cheese and about 3/4 tbsp. (11 mL) green onion on 1/2 of each tortilla to within 1/2 inch (12 mm) of edge. Fold tortillas in half. Carefully transfer to large ungreased baking sheet. Bake in 350°F (175°C) oven for about 10 minutes until crispy. Carefully slide onto cutting board. Makes 6 quesadillas, each cutting into 3 wedges, for a total of 18 wedges.

1 wedge: 132 Calories; 7.6 g Total Fat; 202 mg Sodium; 5 g Protein; 10 g Carbohydrate; 1 g Dietary Fibre

Pictured on page 17 and on back cover.

Variation: For more heat, sprinkle 1 to 2 tsp. (5 to 10 mL) diced pickled jalapeño pepper or banana pepper over cheese.

Strawberry Banana Cooler

Put the whole banana into the refrigerator the night before or into the freezer in the morning while you're getting dressed. You'll have a healthy liquid breakfast in no time! Smooth and creamy.

Milk	1 cup	250 mL
Medium banana, chilled and chopped	1	1
Frozen whole strawberries	2	2
Vanilla	1/2 tsp.	2 mL

Put all 4 ingredients into blender. Process until smooth. Makes about 2 cups (500 mL).

1 cup (250 mL): 115 Calories; 1.7 g Total Fat; 65 mg Sodium; 5 g Protein; 21 g Carbohydrate; 1 g Dietary Fibre

Pictured on page 35.

Coconut Fruit Smoothie

A great breakfast drink for a jump-start to the morning. Taste of the tropics.

Ripe large mango (about 12 oz., 340 g), chopped	1	1
Fresh (or whole frozen) strawberries	10	10
Medium banana (about 5 oz., 140 g), cut up	1	1
Prepared (or freshly squeezed) orange juice	1 cup	250 mL
Light coconut milk	1 cup	250 mL

Put all 5 ingredients into blender. Process until smooth. Makes about 4 cups (1 L).

1 cup (250 mL): 170 Calories; 6.2 g Total Fat; 10 mg Sodium; 3 g Protein; 29 g Carbohydrate; 3 g Dietary Fibre

Pictured on page 17 and on back cover.

Malted Banana Shake

Using bananas which are well ripened makes this creamy, chocolatey drink even better!

Medium bananas	2	2
Malted milk drink powder (such as Ovaltine)	3 tbsp.	50 mL
Frozen vanilla yogurt	2/3 cup	150 mL
Chocolate milk	2 cups	500 mL
Cocoa, sifted if lumpy, sprinkle		

Put first 4 ingredients into blender. Process until smooth.

Sprinkle cocoa over individual servings. Makes 4 cups (1 L).

1 cup (250 mL): 228 Calories; 4.6 g Total Fat; 145 mg Sodium; 7 g Protein; 42 g Carbohydrate; 2 g Dietary Fibre

Pictured on page 18.

Breakfast

Berry Best Shake

Glossy, thick and bright pink! Fresh berry flavours smoothed with vanilla yogurt. Great for a quick snack or breakfast on-the-run.

Vanilla yogurt	1 cup	250 mL
Frozen whole raspberries	1 cup	250 mL
Frozen whole strawberries	1 cup	250 mL
Granulated sugar	1/2 cup	125 mL

Put all 4 ingredients into blender. Process until smooth. Makes 2 1/3 cups (575 mL).

1 cup (250 mL): 342 Calories; 4.1 g Total Fat; 59 mg Sodium; 4 g Protein; 77 g Carbohydrate; 4 g Dietary Fibre

Pictured on page 18.

Pineapple Yogurt Shake

Refreshing, creamy and smooth. A nice drink anytime—not just for breakfast. Garnish with pineapple wedges.

Can of pineapple tidbits, drained and juice reserved	8 oz.	227 mL
Reserved pineapple juice	3 – 4 tbsp.	50 – 60 mL
Plain yogurt	1 cup	250 mL
Liquid honey	2 tbsp.	30 mL
Ground cinnamon	1/4 tsp.	1 mL
Crushed ice	1/2 cup	125 mL

Put all 6 ingredients into blender. Process until smooth. Makes about 2 1/2 cups (625 mL).

1 cup (250 mL): 175 Calories; 1.7 g Total Fat; 74 mg Sodium; 6 g Protein; 37 g Carbohydrate; 1 g Dietary Fibre

Pictured on page 18.

# Shrimp Artichoke Pizza

Gourmet-style pizza in looks and taste. Try adding topping suggestions for even more flavour and colour.

Dijon-flavoured mayonnaise (or mix 2 tsp., 10 mL, honey Dijon mustard with 3 tbsp., 50 mL, mayonnaise)	1/4 cup	60 mL
Cayenne pepper	1/4 tsp.	1 mL
Italian flatbread (or pre-baked pizza crust), 12 inch (30 cm) size	1	1
Can of artichoke hearts, drained, chopped	14 oz.	398 mL
Cooked salad (or cocktail) shrimp, fresh or frozen, thawed (about 4 oz., 113 g)	1/2 cup	125 mL
Grated Asiago cheese	1 1/2 cups	375 mL
Finely sliced green onion	1/3 cup	75 mL

Combine mayonnaise and cayenne pepper in small bowl. Spread on flatbread.

Scatter remaining 4 ingredients, in order given, over mayonnaise mixture. Bake directly on centre rack (or on ungreased 12 inch, 30 cm, pizza pan) in 475°F (240°C) oven for 12 to 14 minutes until cheese is melted and crust is crispy and golden. Cuts into 8 wedges.

1 wedge: 226 Calories; 11.1 g Total Fat; 429 mg Sodium; 12 g Protein; 20 g Carbohydrate; 1 g Dietary Fibre

Variation: Add about 1/2 cup (125 mL) diced, seeded tomato and 1/4 cup (60 mL) sliced ripe olive with artichokes.

 To help keep vegetables and fruit fresh longer, line the vegetable crisper in your refrigerator with a layer of paper towels.

Chicken Pizza

Increase amount of dried crushed chilies to increase the heat!
Lots of mushrooms and garlic. Focaccia makes a different pizza base.
Good with a salad or crunchy coleslaw. You can slice the mushrooms, chop the
basil and grate the mozzarella cheese while the chicken is browning.

Ground chicken	12 oz.	340 g
Chopped onion	1 cup	250 mL
Cooking oil	1 tbsp.	15 mL
Sliced brown (cremini) mushrooms	4 cups	1 L
Garlic cloves, minced (or 1 tsp., 5 mL, powder)	4	4
Dried crushed chilies	1 tsp.	5 mL
Rectangular focaccia bread (8 × 12 inch, 20 × 30 cm, size)	1	1
Pizza sauce	2/3 cup	150 mL
Chopped fresh sweet basil (not dried)	1/3 cup	75 mL
Grated mozzarella cheese	1 cup	250 mL
Finely grated Parmesan cheese	2/3 cup	150 mL
Pepper	1/4 tsp.	1 mL

Scramble-fry ground chicken and onion in cooking oil in large frying pan for 5 to 10 minutes until chicken is lightly browned and onion is soft.

Add mushrooms, garlic and chilies. Sauté for 5 minutes, stirring occasionally, until mushrooms are just soft.

While mushrooms are cooking, cut bread in half horizontally to make 2 layers. Spread pizza sauce on cut sides. Divide and spoon cooked chicken mixture over pizza sauce.

Divide and sprinkle remaining 4 ingredients, in order given, over chicken mixture. Place both halves on ungreased baking sheet. Bake in 475°F (240°C) oven for about 12 minutes until cheese is golden and bread is crispy. Each half cuts into 10 pieces, for a total of 20 pieces.

1 piece: 175 Calories; 6.6 g Total Fat; 265 mg Sodium; 9 g Protein; 20 g Carbohydrate; 1 g Dietary Fibre

Tuna Melt Pizza

Looks as good as it tastes. Dill and tuna are perfect together.
Only a hint of chili—increase for more heat. Moist filling with crunchy base.

Cans of flaked white tuna, packed in water (6 1/2 oz., 184 g, each), drained	2	2
Chopped green onion	1/3 cup	75 mL
Chopped fresh dill (or 1 1/2 tsp., 7 mL, dill weed)	2 tbsp.	30 mL
Mayonnaise (not salad dressing)	3 tbsp.	50 mL
Lemon juice	1 tbsp.	15 mL
Garlic salt	1/2 tsp.	2 mL
Pepper	1/2 tsp.	2 mL
Pre-baked pizza crust (12 inch, 30 cm, size)	1	1
Grated sharp Cheddar cheese	1 cup	250 mL
Dried crushed chilies	1/2 tsp.	2 mL

Combine first 7 ingredients in medium bowl. Spread evenly on pizza crust.

Sprinkle cheese and chilies over tuna mixture. Bake in 475°F (240°C) oven for 12 to 15 minutes until cheese is golden and crust is crispy. Cuts into 8 wedges.

1 wedge: 244 Calories; 11.6 g Total Fat; 529 mg Sodium; 17 g Protein; 17 g Carbohydrate; trace Dietary Fibre

Pictured on page 36.

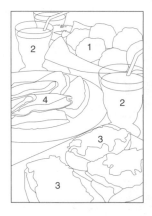

1. Blueberry Muffins, page 33
2. Coconut Fruit Smoothie, page 12
3. Taco Loaf, page 28
4. Breakfast Quesadillas, page 10

Pizza Buns

Great cheese flavour with tomato for added colour.

Hamburger buns, split	2	2
Process cheese spread	4 tsp.	20 mL
Tomato slices	4	4
Salt, sprinkle		
Pepper, sprinkle		
Dried whole oregano, sprinkle		
Grated Parmesan cheese	4 tsp.	20 mL

Arrange bun halves on ungreased baking sheet. Divide and spread cheese spread on each bun half. Divide and lay tomato slices on cheese spread. Sprinkle each with salt, pepper, oregano and Parmesan cheese. Broil 4 inches (10 cm) from heat for 3 to 5 minutes until hot and cheese is melted. Makes 4 bun halves.

1 bun half: 90 Calories; 2.9 g Total Fat; 248 mg Sodium; 4 g Protein; 12 g Carbohydrate; trace Dietary Fibre

1. Pineapple Yogurt Shake, page 13
2. Malted Banana Shake, page 12
3. Berry Best Shake, page 13

Phyllo Pastry Pizza

Good way to use leftover phyllo in freezer. A different pizza base.
Important not to overload it with too much filling. Good lunch or dinner pizza.
Serve with salad.

Frozen phyllo pastry sheets, thawed according to package directions	12	12
Hard margarine (or butter), melted	1/3 cup	75 mL
Deli salami slices (about 1 3/4 oz., 50 g), quartered	8	8
Canned artichoke hearts, drained, thinly sliced	1/3 cup	75 mL
Sliced brown (cremini) mushrooms	1 cup	250 mL
Pimiento-stuffed olives, sliced	2 tbsp.	30 mL
Finely grated Parmesan cheese	3/4 cup	175 mL
Crumbled feta cheese	1/2 cup	125 mL

Lay 1 pastry sheet on ungreased 10 x 15 inch (25 x 38 cm) baking sheet. Do not trim pastry. Press in and up sides of baking sheet. Cover remaining pastry sheets with damp tea towel. Working quickly, brush margarine on pastry sheet. Lay second pastry sheet on top. Press in and up sides. Brush margarine over pastry sheet. Repeat with remaining pastry sheets and margarine.

Scatter next 4 ingredients over pastry.

Sprinkle both cheeses over pizza. Bake in 375°F (190°C) oven for about 15 minutes until cheese is melted and pastry is crispy and golden. Pizza may puff up during baking but will deflate once removed from oven. Cuts into 8 pieces.

1 piece: 254 Calories; 16.5 g Total Fat; 678 mg Sodium; 9 g Protein; 17 g Carbohydrate; 1 g Dietary Fibre

Pictured on page 36.

Paré Pointer
A synonym is the word you use when you can't spell the other one.

Focaccia With Caramelized Onion

The sweetness of onion, the sharpness of smoked cheese and the crunch of the focaccia bread make a tasty combination that tastes great on its own or with a bowl of warming winter soup. You can grate the cheese and chop the thyme while the onion is sautéing.

Medium red onions, sliced	3	3
Olive (or cooking) oil	1 tbsp.	15 mL
Balsamic vinegar	1 tbsp.	15 mL
Brown sugar, packed	2 tbsp.	30 mL
Round focaccia bread (about 9 inches, 22 cm, in diameter), cut horizontally into 2 layers	1	1
Olive (or cooking) oil	2 tsp.	10 mL
Grated applewood smoked (or old) Cheddar cheese	1 cup	250 mL
Chopped fresh thyme leaves (not dried)	1 tbsp.	15 mL
Coarse sea salt	1/2 tsp.	2 mL
Pepper, sprinkle		

Sauté red onion in first amount of olive oil in large frying pan for about 15 minutes, stirring occasionally, until very soft.

Add vinegar. Heat and stir for 1 minute. Add brown sugar. Heat and stir until vinegar is evaporated and brown sugar is dissolved. Cool slightly.

Place bottom half of bread on lightly greased baking sheet. Brush second amount of olive oil on cut side. Spoon onion mixture over bread.

Scatter last 4 ingredients, in order given, over onion mixture. Bake in 450°F (230°C) oven for 5 to 7 minutes until cheese is melted. Top with remaining half of bread. Bake for about 5 minutes until bread is crispy. Cuts into 6 wedges.

1 wedge: 434 Calories; 12.8 g Total Fat; 722 mg Sodium; 14 g Protein; 66 g Carbohydrate; 4 g Dietary Fibre

Mushroom Focaccia

The spinach in the focaccia is a nice alternative to lettuce.
Combination of warm crunchy bread and cool creamy filling
makes a great lunch or light supper.

Sliced brown (cremini) mushrooms (about 11 oz., 310 g)	4 cups	1 L
Olive (or cooking) oil	1 tbsp.	15 mL
Balsamic vinegar	1 tbsp.	15 mL
Brown sugar, packed	1 tsp.	5 mL
Goat cheese, softened	7 oz.	200 g
Finely grated Parmesan cheese	1/3 cup	75 mL
Round focaccia bread (9 1/2 inches, 24 cm, in diameter), cut horizontally into 2 layers	1	1
Pastrami slices (about 12)	10 oz.	285 g
Baby spinach leaves, packed	2 cups	500 mL

Pimiento-stuffed olives, for garnish

Sauté mushrooms in olive oil in large frying pan for 5 to 7 minutes until lightly browned.

Add vinegar and brown sugar. Heat and stir for 2 to 3 minutes until vinegar is evaporated and brown sugar is dissolved.

Combine goat cheese and Parmesan cheese in small bowl. Spread cheese mixture on cut sides of bread.

Layer pastrami, mushroom mixture and spinach on bottom half of bread. Top with remaining half of bread. Transfer to ungreased baking sheet. Bake in 350°F (175°C) oven for about 10 minutes until crisp.

Garnish with olives. Cuts into 8 wedges.

1 wedge: 401 Calories; 14.7 g Total Fat; 959 mg Sodium; 21 g Protein; 46 g Carbohydrate; 3 g Dietary Fibre

Pictured on front cover.

Chicken Salad Subs

Crunchy, creamy texture. Bountiful filling. Great way to use leftover chicken or a pre-cooked chicken from the store. This may be the best chicken salad sandwich that you have ever had. A unique way of using a baguette.

Sour cream	1/4 cup	60 mL
Mayonnaise (not salad dressing)	1/4 cup	60 mL
Dijon mustard	2 tbsp.	30 mL
Chopped cooked chicken	1 2/3 cups	400 mL
Chopped green onion	3/4 cup	175 mL
Finely chopped red pepper	3/4 cup	175 mL
Finely chopped celery	1/4 cup	60 mL
Salt	1/4 tsp.	1 mL
Pepper	1/4 tsp.	1 mL
Baguette bread loaf (about 21 inches, 53 cm, in length)	1	1

Combine sour cream, mayonnaise and mustard in medium bowl.

Add next 6 ingredients. Mix well.

Cut ends from loaf. Cut remaining loaf into 4 pieces crosswise. Cut each piece almost through horizontally, being careful not to cut through to the other side. Fill each piece with chicken salad mixture. Makes 4 subs.

1 sub: 399 Calories; 17.6 g Total Fat; 692 mg Sodium; 25 g Protein; 34 g Carbohydrate; 3 g Dietary Fibre

Maintain an ongoing 'staples' grocery list, kept in a handy location in the kitchen, that family members can add to as they use up items such as milk, cheese, eggs, bread, cookies, pickles, peanut butter and so on. These are the items that the cook assumes are always in the cupboard or refrigerator and are often the items that are lifesavers at rushed mealtimes. However, these are also the items that everyone seems to 'snack' on throughout the week so the cook is never quite sure what is or isn't needed. And remember — keep a pencil tied to the list too, so there are no excuses!

Bacon And Sun-Dried Tomato Sandwiches

Very colourful and really delicious! Bacon adds smoky flavour.
Serve for lunch as is or for dinner with soup.

Bacon slices	12	12
Block of cream cheese, softened	4 oz.	125 g
Honey Dijon mustard	3 tbsp.	50 mL
Chopped fresh chives (or 2 1/2 tsp., 12 mL, dried)	3 tbsp.	50 mL
French bread loaf slices, cut 1 inch (2.5 cm) thick	8	8
Ripe avocado, sliced	1	1
Sun-dried tomatoes in oil, drained, sliced	12	12

Fry bacon in large frying pan for about 10 minutes until crisp. Drain well on paper towels. Cool.

While bacon is frying, combine cream cheese, mustard and chives in small bowl.

Spread cream cheese mixture on one side of each bread slice.

Layer avocado, cooled bacon and sun-dried tomato on cream cheese mixture on half of bread slices. Cover with remaining bread slices. Makes 4 sandwiches.

1 sandwich: 522 Calories; 32.1 g Total Fat; 1008 mg Sodium; 17 g Protein; 44 g Carbohydrate; 3 g Dietary Fibre

Pictured on page 53.

Paré Pointer
Astronauts can't go to the moon when it's full.

Tomato Cheese Sandwich

This open-faced sandwich is pale orange in colour with
tomato pieces showing. Spiced just right. A quick brunch or lunch meal.

Finely chopped onion	1/4 cup	60 mL
Hard margarine (or butter)	1 tsp.	5 mL
Large egg	1	1
Medium tomato, diced	1	1
Grated medium (or sharp) Cheddar cheese	3 tbsp.	50 mL
Dried whole oregano	1/8 tsp.	0.5 mL
Dried sweet basil	1/8 tsp.	0.5 mL
Pepper	1/8 tsp.	0.5 mL
Whole wheat kaiser rolls, cut in half (buttered, optional)	2	2

Sliced grape tomatoes, for garnish
Fresh basil sprig, for garnish

Sauté onion in margarine in medium frying pan for 3 to 5 minutes until soft.

While onion is cooking, beat egg with fork in small bowl. Add next 5 ingredients. Mix. Add to softened onion. Heat and stir for 2 minutes until egg is cooked. Mixture will be moist because of the tomato. Makes 3/4 cup (175 mL) filling.

Spread 3 tbsp. (50 mL) filling on each bun half.

Garnish with tomato and basil. Makes 4 bun halves.

1 bun half: 121 Calories; 5.2 g Total Fat; 184 mg Sodium; 5 g Protein; 14 g Carbohydrate; 1 g Dietary Fibre

Pictured on page 53.

Pictured on page 53.

Paré Pointer
When your food tastes like soap, you know the
cafeteria's kitchen is clean.

Bunwich Broil

Toasty on the inside and soft on the outside. Good ham and cheese flavour with a hint of sweetness from relish. Quick to make one or several at the same time. Great for lunch with a side salad!

Sweet pickle relish	1 tsp.	5 mL
Prepared mustard (optional)	1/2 tsp.	2 mL
English muffin (or hamburger bun), split (buttered optional)	1	1
Deli ham slice, chopped	1	1
Process Cheddar cheese slice	1	1

Spread relish and mustard on bottom half of muffin. Cover with ham and cheese. Place both muffin halves on small ungreased baking sheet. Broil 4 inches (10 cm) from heat until cheese is melted and muffins are toasted. Place top half of muffin over cheese. Serves 1.

1 serving: 321 Calories; 14.5 g Total Fat; 1216 mg Sodium; 18 g Protein; 30 g Carbohydrate; 0 g Dietary Fibre

Crab Filling

Use to fill toasted multi-grain bread, warmed flour or whole wheat pitas or croissants. To complete the sandwich, add green leaf lettuce. Filling can be made ahead and stored in refrigerator until ready to assemble.

Cans of crabmeat (4 1/2 oz., 120 g, each), drained, cartilage removed (or about 1 1/2 cups, 375 mL, imitation crabmeat)	2	2
Small roma (plum) tomatoes, seeded and diced	2	2
Finely sliced green onion	2 tbsp.	30 mL
Finely diced celery	2 tbsp.	30 mL
Ranch (or Caesar salad) dressing	1/3 cup	75 mL

(continued on next page)

Combine first 4 ingredients in medium bowl.

Pour dressing over crab mixture. Toss until lightly coated. Makes about 2 cups (500 mL).

1/2 cup (125 mL): 162 Calories; 11.2 g Total Fat; 394 mg Sodium; 12 g Protein; 3 g Carbohydrate; 1 g Dietary Fibre

Pictured on page 71.

Barbecued Beef Buns

Perfect for the leftover roast beef in the refrigerator.
Or pick up some deli beef at the supermarket on your way home.

Medium onion, thinly sliced	1	1
Hard margarine (or butter)	1 tbsp.	15 mL
Barbecue sauce	2/3 cup	150 mL
Chili sauce	1/3 cup	75 mL
Lemon juice	1 tbsp.	15 mL
Brown sugar, packed	2 tbsp.	30 mL
Worcestershire sauce	1 tsp.	5 mL
Thinly sliced cooked (or deli) roast beef	17 1/2 oz.	500 g
Oval crusty (or Italian) rolls, cut in half	6	6

Sauté onion in margarine in large frying pan until soft and beginning to turn golden.

Add next 5 ingredients. Stir. Bring to a simmer.

While onion mixture is heating, cut beef crosswise into strips. Add to onion mixture. Stir until heated through. Makes 3 1/2 cups (875 mL) filling.

Place 1/2 cup (125 mL) filling on each of 6 bun halves. Top with remaining bun halves. Makes 6 beef buns.

1 beef bun: 390 Calories; 9.4 g Total Fat; 853 mg Sodium; 31 g Protein; 44 g Carbohydrate; 3 g Dietary Fibre

Taco Loaf

Tastes just like a taco. Loaf is a novel idea—a pleasing change from typical tortillas. You can chop the peppers, tomato and green onion while the ground beef is cooking. Grating the cheese directly over the loaves saves time and clean up.

Lean ground beef	1 lb.	454 g
Chopped onion	1/2 cup	125 mL
Chopped green pepper	1/2 cup	125 mL
Chopped red pepper	1/2 cup	125 mL
Jar of bean dip	9 oz.	255 g
Can of diced green chilies	4 oz.	113 g
Envelope of taco seasoning mix	1 1/4 oz.	35 g
French bread loaf, cut in half lengthwise	1	1
Diced tomato	1/2 cup	125 mL
Sliced green onion	1/4 cup	60 mL
Grated Cheddar (or mozzarella or Monterey Jack With Jalapeño) cheese	1 cup	250 mL

Scramble-fry ground beef and onion in medium frying pan for about 5 minutes until beef is no longer pink. Add both peppers. Sauté for 2 minutes. Drain.

Add bean dip, green chilies and taco seasoning. Cook for 2 to 3 minutes, stirring often, until heated through.

Divide and spread beef mixture on each loaf half. Transfer to ungreased baking sheet.

Divide and sprinkle tomato, green onion and cheese over beef mixture. Broil about 8 inches (20 cm) from heat for 1 to 2 minutes until hot and cheese is melted. Each half cuts into 6 to 8 pieces, for a total of 12 to 16 pieces.

1 piece: 237 Calories; 7.9 g Total Fat; 641 mg Sodium; 14 g Protein; 27 g Carbohydrate; 3 g Dietary Fibre

Pictured on page 17 and on back cover.

Open-Faced Shrimp Loaf

Cheesy and creamy. Onion enhances the flavour. Serve with a salad.
Take the cream cheese out of the refrigerator in the morning or soften quickly
in microwave while opening and draining the can of shrimp.

Block of cream cheese, softened	8 oz.	250 g
Lemon juice	1 tbsp.	15 mL
Milk	1/4 cup	60 mL
Ketchup	1 tsp.	5 mL
Minced onion flakes	4 tsp.	20 mL
Prepared horseradish	1/2 tsp.	2 mL
Can of cocktail shrimp, drained (or about 1 cup, 250 mL, cooked salad shrimp)	3 1/2 oz.	100 g
French bread loaf, cut in half lengthwise	1	1

Salt, sprinkle
Pepper, sprinkle
Parsley flakes, sprinkle

Mash cream cheese, lemon juice, milk and ketchup together in medium bowl.

Mix in onion flakes, horseradish and shrimp. Makes 1 2/3 cups (400 mL) filling.

Divide and spread filling on each loaf half. Transfer to ungreased baking sheet. Broil about 7 inches (18 cm) from heat for about 5 minutes, turning pan at half time, until hot and lightly browned.

Sprinkle salt, pepper and parsley over filling. Cuts into 16 pieces.

1 piece: 143 Calories; 6.5 g Total Fat; 236 mg Sodium; 5 g Protein; 16 g Carbohydrate; 1 g Dietary Fibre

Paré Pointer
If you have two bananas, you have a pair of slippers.

Shrimp And Asparagus Wraps

Fresh and spring-like.

Fresh thin asparagus, trimmed of tough ends (cut thick spears in half lengthwise)	1/2 lb.	225 g
Boiling water		
Ice water		
Frozen cooked medium shrimp (peeled and deveined), thawed	1 lb.	454 g
Mayonnaise (not salad dressing)	1/3 cup	75 mL
Wasabi paste (Japanese horseradish)	2 tsp.	10 mL
Large flour (or basil pesto) tortillas (about 10 inches, 25 cm), see Tip, page 8	4	4
Thinly sliced red onion	1/4 cup	60 mL

Cook asparagus in boiling water in large saucepan for about 3 minutes until tender-crisp. Drain. Put into large bowl of ice water. Let stand for 5 to 7 minutes until cold. Drain.

While asparagus is cooling, cut shrimp in half lengthwise. Set aside.

Combine mayonnaise and wasabi paste in small bowl. Divide and spread on 1 side of tortillas.

Layer asparagus, shrimp and red onion slices, in order given, down centre of each tortilla to within 2 inches (5 cm) of bottom edge. Fold bottom edge up over filling. Roll up, jelly roll-style, from sides. Slice in half diagonally. Makes 4 wraps, each cutting into 2, for a total of 8 halves.

1 half: 205 Calories; 10.3 g Total Fat; 236 mg Sodium; 14 g Protein; 14 g Carbohydrate; 1 g Dietary Fibre

Pictured on page 53.

Pizza Wraps

Tastes just like a pizza. Great for a snack or meal. Kids will love these!

Can of pizza sauce	7 1/2 oz.	213 mL
Large flour tortillas (about 10 inches, 25 cm), see Tip, page 8	4	4
Chopped cooked (or deli) ham	1/2 cup	125 mL
Slivered pepperoni (about 16 slices)	1/2 cup	125 mL
Medium red pepper, slivered	1	1
Small red onion, sliced	1	1
Sliced ripe olives	1/4 cup	60 mL
Pineapple tidbits, well drained	1/3 cup	75 mL
Grated medium Cheddar cheese	1/3 cup	75 mL
Grated mozzarella cheese	1/4 cup	60 mL
Finely grated Parmesan cheese	1/4 cup	60 mL

Divide and spread pizza sauce on 1 side of each tortilla.

Layer next 9 ingredients, in order given, down centre of each tortilla to within 2 inches (5 cm) of bottom edge. Fold bottom edge over filling. Roll up from 1 side to enclose filling, leaving top open. Arrange tortillas, seam side down, on ungreased baking sheet. Bake in 375°F (190°C) oven for about 15 minutes until lightly browned and crisp. Makes 4 wraps.

1 wrap: 572 Calories; 34.4 g Total Fat; 1918 mg Sodium; 26 g Protein; 40 g Carbohydrate; 3 g Dietary Fibre

 Include the entire family in meal preparation. Assign tasks so everyone can help with getting the food on the table faster. Older children can clean the vegetables while the younger ones can set the table. Don't forget to enlist help with cleanup too!

Cherry Almond Muffins

These muffins are a golden colour and have a nice almond flavour.
For even faster preparation, combine and cover dry ingredients in
the morning, or even the night before, until ready to add wet
ingredients just before baking. Toast almonds ahead of time too.

All-purpose flour	2 cups	500 mL
Baking powder	1 tbsp.	15 mL
Salt	1/2 tsp.	2 mL
Dried cherries	1 cup	250 mL
Hard margarine (or butter), softened	1/4 cup	60 mL
Granulated sugar	1/3 cup	75 mL
Large egg	1	1
Milk	3/4 cup	175 mL
Almond flavouring	1/2 tsp.	2 mL

TOPPING

Granulated sugar	1 tbsp.	15 mL
Ground almonds, toasted (see Tip, page 42)	1/4 cup	60 mL

Combine flour, baking powder, salt and cherries in large bowl. Make a well in centre.

Cream margarine and sugar together in medium bowl. Beat in egg. Add milk and flavouring. Stir. Pour into well. Stir until just moistened. Fill greased muffin cups 3/4 full.

Topping: Combine sugar and almonds in small bowl. Sprinkle over muffin batter. Bake in 400°F (205°C) oven for 18 to 20 minutes until wooden pick inserted in centre of muffin comes out clean. Let stand in pan for 5 minutes before removing to wire rack to cool. Makes 12 muffins.

1 muffin: 202 Calories; 6.1 g Total Fat; 253 mg Sodium; 4 g Protein; 34 g Carbohydrate; 1 g Dietary Fibre

Pictured on page 35.

BLUEBERRY ALMOND MUFFINS: Omit dried cherries. Add about 2/3 cup (150 mL) dried blueberries.

Blueberry Muffins

A hearty, satisfying muffin filled with berries. Great for a breakfast item.

All-purpose flour	1 1/4 cups	300 mL
Quick-cooking rolled oats (not instant)	1 cup	250 mL
Baking powder	2 tsp.	10 mL
Baking soda	1/2 tsp.	2 mL
Salt	1/2 tsp.	2 mL
Hard margarine (or butter), softened	1/4 cup	60 mL
Brown sugar, packed	2/3 cup	150 mL
Large eggs	2	2
Sour cream	1 cup	250 mL
Dried blueberries	1 cup	250 mL

Stir first 5 ingredients together in large bowl. Make a well in centre.

Cream margarine and brown sugar together in medium bowl. Beat in eggs, 1 at a time, beating well after each addition. Add sour cream. Mix. Pour into well. Stir until just moistened.

Gently stir in blueberries. Fill greased muffin cups 3/4 full. Bake in 400°F (205°C) oven for 15 to 20 minutes until wooden pick inserted in centre of muffin comes out clean. Let stand in pan for 5 minutes before turning out onto wire rack to cool. Makes 12 muffins.

1 muffin: 241 Calories; 8.6 g Total Fat; 290 mg Sodium; 5 g Protein; 37 g Carbohydrate; 3 g Dietary Fibre

Pictured on page 17 and on back cover.

Paré Pointer

That Newfoundland bird is always out of breath. He's a puffin.

Pesto Parmesan Toasts

The family will come a runnin' once the smell of these toasts begins to waft through the house. Parmesan and pesto make a wonderful match. A slightly different addition as a bread to serve with lunch or the evening meal.

Loaf of ciabatta (or French) bread (about 9 inches, 22 cm, in length), cut into 3/4 inch (2 cm) thick slices	1	1
Basil pesto	6 tbsp.	100 mL
Finely grated Parmesan cheese	6 tbsp.	100 mL
Pepper	1/4 tsp.	1 mL

Arrange bread slices in single layer on ungreased baking sheet. Bake in 350°F (175°C) oven for about 5 minutes per side until lightly browned.

Spread pesto on 1 side of each bread slice. Sprinkle Parmesan cheese and pepper over pesto. Broil about 5 inches (12.5 cm) from heat for 2 to 3 minutes until cheese is melted and slightly golden. Makes 12 slices.

1 slice: 177 Calories; 4.4 g Total Fat; 258 mg Sodium; 5 g Protein; 29 g Carbohydrate; 1 g Dietary Fibre

Pictured on page 54.

1. Cherry Almond Muffins, page 32
2. Strawberry Banana Cooler, page 11
3. One-Dish Eggs, page 8

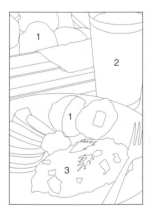

Parmesan Drop Biscuits

Golden, moist biscuits dotted with flecks of parsley and paprika.
Crusty on the outside and soft on the inside. Very simple to make.

All-purpose flour	1 1/2 cups	375 mL
Baking powder	2 tsp.	10 mL
Parsley flakes	2 tsp.	10 mL
Grated Parmesan cheese	3 tbsp.	50 mL
Hard margarine (or butter), cut into 6 pieces	1/3 cup	75 mL
Milk	3/4 cup	175 mL

Paprika, sprinkle

Put first 5 ingredients into food processor. Pulse with on/off motion until margarine resembles coarse bread crumbs. Transfer to medium bowl.

Add milk. Stir until just moistened and dough is sticky. Drop by large spoonfuls, about 12, onto greased baking sheet.

Sprinkle paprika over dough. Bake on centre rack in 425°F (220°C) oven for 12 minutes until golden. Makes 12 biscuits.

1 biscuit: 122 Calories; 6.2 g Total Fat; 162 mg Sodium; 3 g Protein; 14 g Carbohydrate; 1 g Dietary Fibre

1. Tuna Melt Pizza, page 16
2. Chicken Tacos, page 87
3. Phyllo Pastry Pizza, page 20

Props Courtesy Of: Browne & Co. Ltd.

Crusty Cheese Biscuits

Good with Barley Beef Soup, page 145, chilies and casseroles.
Especially good warm.

All-purpose flour	4 cups	1 L
Baking powder	2 tbsp.	30 mL
Salt	2 tsp.	10 mL
Hard margarine (or butter)	2 tbsp.	30 mL
Finely grated Parmesan cheese	1/3 cup	75 mL
Dried rosemary	1 tsp.	5 mL
Buttermilk (or reconstituted from powder)	2 cups	500 mL
Grainy mustard	2 tbsp.	30 mL
Finely grated Parmesan cheese	1/3 cup	75 mL

Combine flour, baking powder and salt in large bowl. Cut in margarine until crumbly.

Add first amount of Parmesan cheese and rosemary. Mix well. Make a well in centre.

Combine buttermilk and mustard in 2 cup (500 mL) liquid measure. Pour into well. Mix with fork until just moistened and dough is sticky. Turn out onto lightly floured surface. Gently knead 3 or 4 times until mixture comes together. Do not over knead. Press out dough to 3/4 inch (2 cm) thickness. Cut out 2 3/4 inch (7 cm) rounds from dough using lightly floured cutter.

Place rounds, just touching, in greased 9 × 13 inch (22 × 33 cm) pan. Sprinkle with second amount of Parmesan cheese. Bake in 400°F (205°C) oven for about 20 minutes until golden brown. Makes about 12 biscuits.

1 biscuit: 219 Calories; 4.7 g Total Fat; 793 mg Sodium; 8 g Protein; 35 g Carbohydrate;
1 g Dietary Fibre

Pictured on page 72.

Sour Milk Biscuits

Light, flaky texture in these basic biscuits. Try the variations below to add a bit of interest—but remember, time will be added as well.

Milk	3/4 cup	175 mL
White vinegar	1 tbsp.	15 mL
All-purpose flour	2 cups	500 mL
Salt	3/4 tsp.	4 mL
Baking soda	1/2 tsp.	2 mL
Hard margarine (or butter)	6 tbsp.	100 mL

Pour milk into 1 cup (250 mL) liquid measure. Add vinegar. Stir.

Stir flour, salt and baking soda together in medium bowl. Cut in margarine until mixture resembles coarse bread crumbs. Make a well in centre. Add milk mixture. Stir to form ball. Turn out onto lightly floured surface. Gently knead 6 times. Pat or roll out to 1/2 inch (12 mm) thickness. Cut into 2 inch (5 cm) rounds with lightly floured cutter. Arrange, about 2 inches (5 cm) apart, on greased baking sheet. Bake in 450°F (230°C) oven for 12 to 15 minutes until risen and golden. Makes 16 biscuits.

1 biscuit: 104 Calories; 4.6 g Total Fat; 209 mg Sodium; 2 g Protein; 13 g Carbohydrate; 1 g Dietary Fibre

Variation: Add 1 finely chopped green onion to flour mixture.

Variation: Add 1/2 cup (125 mL) grated sharp Cheddar cheese or Monterey Jack With Jalapeño cheese to flour mixture.

Variation: Add 1 tbsp. (15 mL) crushed flaxseed or sunflower seeds to flour mixture.

 To get a head start on your next scratch cake, batch of cookies or pan of biscuits, make up two or three recipes of the dry ingredients ahead of time. Put into a jar or other airtight container. Tuck in a copy of the complete recipe. Label jar with the recipe name and the measured amount for one recipe. Store container in the cupboard.

Grilled Vegetable Salad

Bright and colourful. Mediterranean flavours that are good, warm or cold.
Serve with Wingin' It Wings, page 91.

Medium red peppers	2	2
Medium eggplant (about 1 lb., 454 g)	1	1
Medium zucchini	2	2
Olive (or cooking) oil	2 tbsp.	30 mL
Baguette bread (about 22 inches, 56 cm)	1/2	1/2
Olive (or cooking) oil	2 tbsp.	30 mL
Can of artichoke hearts, drained, quartered	14 oz.	398 mL
Pine nuts, toasted (see Tip, page 42)	1/3 cup	75 mL
GARLIC DRESSING		
Olive (or cooking) oil	2/3 cup	150 mL
Red wine vinegar	1/4 cup	60 mL
Garlic cloves	4	4
Granulated sugar	2 tbsp.	30 mL
Salt	1/2 tsp.	2 mL
Pepper	1/2 tsp.	2 mL

Preheat barbecue to medium. While barbecue is heating, cut peppers into quarters. Cook peppers on greased grill over medium heat for 8 to 10 minutes until skin is blistered and blackened. Cover with plastic wrap. Let sweat for 10 minutes until cool enough to handle. Scrape off and discard skin from peppers. Cut peppers into 1/2 inch (12 mm) thick strips.

While peppers are grilling, peel and cut eggplant into 1/4 inch (6 mm) slices. Cut zucchini, with peel, into 1/4 inch (6 mm) slices. Brush both sides of eggplant and zucchini slices with first amount of olive oil. Cook on greased grill, beside peppers, over medium heat for 3 to 5 minutes per side until browned. Coarsely chop peppers, eggplant and zucchini. Put into large serving bowl.

Cut baguette into 20 slices. Brush both sides of each slice with second amount of olive oil. Cook on greased grill, beside vegetables, over medium heat for about 2 minutes per side until lightly browned. Cut slices in half. Add to vegetable mixture in bowl.

(continued on next page)

Add artichoke hearts and pine nuts to vegetable mixture. Toss.

Garlic Dressing: Put all 6 ingredients into blender. Process until smooth. Makes 2/3 cup (150 mL) dressing. Drizzle over vegetable mixture. Toss. Makes 8 cups (2 L).

1 cup (250 mL): 369 Calories; 30.2 g Total Fat; 356 mg Sodium; 6 g Protein; 24 g Carbohydrate; 4 g Dietary Fibre

Pictured on page 125.

Matilda Salad

Hot potato salad made the Australian way. Nice creamy texture. Excellent flavour. The mix of ingredients is lovely.

Cubed potato	5 cups	1.25 L
Diced celery	1 cup	250 mL
Chopped onion	1 cup	250 mL
Water	2 cups	500 mL
Salt	1 tsp.	5 mL
DRESSING		
Mayonnaise	1/2 cup	125 mL
Sour cream	1/2 cup	125 mL
Cooking oil	3 tbsp.	50 mL
White vinegar	1 tbsp.	15 mL
Salt	1/2 tsp.	2 mL

Put potato, celery, onion, water and salt into large saucepan. Bring to a boil. Cover. Reduce heat. Simmer for about 20 minutes, stirring occasionally, until potato is tender. Drain.

Dressing: While potato mixture is cooking, mix mayonnaise and sour cream in small bowl. Add cooking oil, vinegar and salt. Stir. Makes 1 1/4 cups (300 mL) dressing. Pour over drained potato mixture. Mix gently until coated. Serve hot. Makes 5 cups (1.25 L). Serves 6.

1 serving: 352 Calories; 25.5 g Total Fat; 730 mg Sodium; 4 g Protein; 28 g Carbohydrate; 3 g Dietary Fibre

Pickled Beet Salad

Vibrant colours. Slightly bitter endive combines well with sweet pickled beets. Serve on a bed of crisp, torn romaine for an extra special presentation. Goes well with beef dishes. Put a slow cooker stew on in the morning, and make the salad when you get home. Or serve with Tarragon-Topped Fish, page 95.

Jar of sliced pickled beets, drained, cut julienne	26 oz.	750 mL
Italian dressing	1/2 cup	125 mL
Belgian endive leaves (about 4 oz., 125 g, each), shredded	2	2
Small radicchio leaf (about 6 oz., 170 g), shredded	1	1
Romaine lettuce hearts, torn (optional)	2	2
Pepper, sprinkle		

Gently combine beets and dressing in large bowl.

Add endive and radicchio. Toss.

Divide romaine lettuce among 6 salad plates. Top each with about 1 cup (250 mL) beet mixture. Sprinkle pepper over top. Serves 6.

1 serving: 221 Calories; 14.5 g Total Fat; 650 mg Sodium; 2 g Protein; 24 g Carbohydrate; 2 g Dietary Fibre

Pictured on page 54.

BLUE CHEESE AND BEET SALAD: Top above salad with about 1/2 cup (125 mL) crumbled blue cheese.

 To toast nuts and seeds, place in ungreased frying pan. Heat on medium, stirring constantly, until lightly browned. Packages of pre-toasted sesame seeds are sometimes available in the produce section.

Salad Mix

Serve immediately to keep the salad greens crisp. Seeds add a nuttiness that goes very well with the cheese. Garnish with additional sesame seeds and grated Parmesan cheese if you have the time. Serve with Chicken Cacciatore, page 92, or Pineapple Steak, page 142.

Bag of mixed salad greens (about 6 cups, 1.5 L)	10 oz.	283 g
Sesame seeds, toasted (see Tip, page 42)	1 tbsp.	15 mL
Grated Parmesan cheese	2 tbsp.	30 mL
Italian dressing	1/4 cup	60 mL

Toss salad greens, sesame seeds and Parmesan cheese in large bowl.

Drizzle dressing over salad green mixture. Toss well. Makes 6 cups (1.5 L).

1 cup (250 mL): 91 Calories; 8.7 g Total Fat; 216 mg Sodium; 2 g Protein; 2 g Carbohydrate; 1 g Dietary Fibre

Dairy Salad

Dash home at lunchtime and whip this salad together. Serve with a bun and some fresh fruit.

Creamed cottage cheese	3/4 cup	175 mL
Sour cream	1/2 cup	125 mL
Salt	1/4 tsp.	1 mL
Pepper	1/8 tsp.	0.5 mL
Chopped fresh dill (or 1/8 tsp., 0.5 mL, dill weed)	1/2 tsp.	2 mL
Medium English cucumber (about 12 oz., 340 g), with peel, diced	3/4 cup	175 mL
Green onion, thinly sliced	1/2	1/2

Combine first 5 ingredients in medium bowl.

Add cucumber and green onion. Stir. Makes 2 cups (500 mL).

1/2 cup (125 mL): 190 Calories; 12.4 g Total Fat; 661 mg Sodium; 13 g Protein; 7 g Carbohydrate; 1 g Dietary Fibre

Fresh Fruit Salad

Dressing is light with a soft citrus flavour. The mixed greens, topped with a nice buttery yellow dressing, are a pretty colour combination.

CREAMY DRESSING

Frozen concentrated orange juice	3 tbsp.	50 mL
Lemon juice	1 tbsp.	15 mL
Dijon mustard	1/2 tsp.	2 mL
Non-fat plain yogurt	3/4 cup	175 mL
Liquid honey	2 tbsp.	30 mL
Ground cinnamon, just a pinch		
Ground cloves, just a pinch		
Mixed salad greens, lightly packed	4 cups	1 L
Ripe pears, peeled, cored and thinly sliced	2	2
Fresh strawberries, stems removed and sliced in half	8	8
Fresh raspberries (or blueberries)	1 cup	250 mL

Creamy Dressing: Combine first 7 ingredients in small bowl. Makes 1 cup (250 mL) dressing. Cover. Chill while preparing and arranging salad.

Divide salad greens among 4 salad plates. Arrange pears, strawberries and raspberries in attractive design on salad greens. Drizzle 2 to 3 tbsp. (30 to 50 mL) dressing over each fruit mixture. Serve remaining dressing on the side. Serves 4.

1 serving: 137 Calories; 0.6 g Total Fat; 62 mg Sodium; 4 g Protein; 31 g Carbohydrate; 5 g Dietary Fibre

Pictured on page 54.

Paré Pointer
She said she got an "A" in spelling, but there is no "A" in spelling!

Mild Curry Chicken Salad

This meal-type salad has lots of crunchy texture. Dressing is thick and coats well. Peanut and curry flavours, while slightly sweet.

Boneless, skinless chicken breast halves (about 4), diced	1 lb.	454 g
Cooking oil	1 tbsp.	15 mL
Bag of mixed salad greens, chopped (about 6 cups, 1.5 L)	10 oz.	283 g
Shredded cabbage	1 cup	250 mL
Thinly sliced celery	1/2 cup	125 mL
Thinly sliced red onion (optional)	1/2 cup	125 mL
Can of apricot halves, drained, juice reserved	14 oz.	398 mL
Peanuts	1/2 cup	125 mL
MILD CURRY DRESSING		
Sour cream	1/2 cup	125 mL
Smooth peanut butter	1/4 cup	60 mL
Reserved apricot juice	1/3 cup	75 mL
White vinegar	1 tbsp.	15 mL
Granulated sugar	1 tsp.	5 mL
Curry powder	3/4 tsp.	4 mL
Onion powder	1/8 tsp.	0.5 mL
Salt	1/4 – 1/2 tsp.	1 – 2 mL

Sauté chicken in cooking oil in medium frying pan for about 8 minutes until no pink remains. Spread out on baking sheet to cool quickly.

Meanwhile, put salad greens into large bowl. Add cabbage, celery, onion, apricots and peanuts. Toss.

Mild Curry Dressing: Mix all 8 ingredients well in small bowl. Makes 1 cup (250 mL) dressing. Pour over salad mixture. Add chicken. Toss to coat. Makes 8 cups (2 L). Serves 4.

1 serving: 492 Calories; 28.3 g Total Fat; 283 mg Sodium; 38 g Protein; 27 g Carbohydrate; 6 g Dietary Fibre

Seafood Salad

Great salad to serve as a meal. Appealing mixture of colours and textures. Can taste all ingredients, as dressing only enhances rather than masks the fresh flavours. Fresh pasta cooks faster than dry.

Fresh linguine (or other) pasta, cut into 1 1/2 inch (3.8 cm) pieces	8 oz.	225 g
Frozen mixed peas and carrots	1 cup	250 mL
Boiling water	12 cups	3 L
Salt	2 tsp.	10 mL
Bag of romaine lettuce, chopped (about 6 cups, 1.5 L)	10 oz.	285 g
Green onions, chopped	2	2
Grated medium Cheddar cheese	1/2 cup	125 mL
Crabmeat (or imitation crabmeat), coarsely chopped	1 cup	250 mL
Cooked salad shrimp (or one 3.5 oz., 100 g, can of cocktail shrimp)	1 cup	250 mL
Finely slivered red pepper	1/4 cup	60 mL
HORSERADISH DRESSING		
Salad dressing (or mayonnaise)	1/2 cup	125 mL
White vinegar	1 tbsp.	15 mL
Prepared horseradish	1 1/2 tsp.	7 mL
Salt	3/4 tsp.	4 mL
Pepper, sprinkle		

Cook pasta and peas and carrots in boiling water and salt in large uncovered pot or Dutch oven for about 4 minutes until pasta is tender but firm. Drain. Rinse with cold water. Drain. Cool.

While pasta is cooking, combine next 6 ingredients in large bowl. Add pasta. Toss.

Horseradish Dressing: Stir all 5 ingredients together well in small bowl. Makes about 1/2 cup (125 mL) dressing. Pour over lettuce mixture. Toss. Makes 8 cups (2 L). Serves 4 as a main salad.

1 serving: 532 Calories; 22.2 g Total Fat; 1074 mg Sodium; 29 g Protein; 53 g Carbohydrate; 4 g Dietary Fibre

Pictured on page 54.

Tex-Mex Salad

*This is a bright, colourful and crunchy salad—perfect to feed a
crowd that's in a hurry. A meal in itself.*

Chopped cooked chicken (see Note)	3 1/2 cups	875 mL
Can of kernel corn, drained	12 oz.	341 mL
Can of black beans, rinsed and drained	19 oz.	540 mL
Chopped red onion	2 cups	500 mL
Halved grape (or cherry) tomatoes	2 1/2 cups	625 mL
Ripe avocado, peeled, pitted and chopped	1	1
Coarsely chopped romaine lettuce	5 cups	1.25 L
SALSA DRESSING		
Salsa	1/2 cup	125 mL
Olive (or cooking) oil	1/4 cup	60 mL
Balsamic vinegar	2 tbsp.	30 mL
Sour cream	2 tbsp.	30 mL
Tortilla (or corn) chips	3 cups	750 mL

Combine first 7 ingredients in large serving bowl.

Salsa Dressing: Combine first 4 ingredients in jar with tight-fitting lid.
Shake well. Makes 3/4 cup (175 mL) dressing. Drizzle over chicken
mixture.

Add tortilla chips. Toss. Makes about 14 cups (3.5 L).

*1 cup (250 mL): 188 Calories; 9.4 g Total Fat; 171 mg Sodium; 14 g Protein; 13 g Carbohydrate;
2 g Dietary Fibre*

Pictured on front cover.

Note: If you don't have leftover chicken, stop at the deli on your way
home and pick up a pre-cooked whole chicken. Remove meat. Discard skin
and bones. Chop meat. Add about 5 minutes to the total time.

Speedy Chef's Salad

Stop in at the deli on your way home to pick up the meat and buns. Keep hard-boiled eggs on hand in the refrigerator. Colourful and refreshing meal-type salad with a light vinaigrette dressing. Serve with a basket of multi-grain buns.

Medium head of lettuce (or assorted greens), cut bite size (about 8 cups, 2 L)	1	1
Cooked turkey (or chicken) slices, cut into strips	2 3/4 oz.	75 g
Cooked beef slices, cut into strips	2 3/4 oz.	75 g
Cooked ham slices, cut into strips	2 3/4 oz.	75 g
Thinly sliced and slivered radishes	1/4 cup	60 mL
Diced medium Cheddar cheese	1/2 cup	125 mL
Cherry tomatoes, halved	12	12
Hard-boiled eggs, chopped	4	4
APPLE CIDER DRESSING		
Apple cider vinegar	1/3 cup	75 mL
Cooking oil	1/4 cup	60 mL
Granulated sugar	1 1/2 tsp.	7 mL
Grated onion	1 tbsp.	15 mL

Put lettuce into large bowl.

Add meat strips to lettuce.

Add next 4 ingredients. Toss.

Apple Cider Dressing: Stir first 4 ingredients in small bowl until sugar is dissolved. Makes 2/3 cup (150 mL) dressing. Pour over lettuce mixture. Toss. Divide among 4 dinner plates. Serves 4.

1 serving: 403 Calories; 29.5 g Total Fat; 478 mg Sodium; 27 g Protein; 8 g Carbohydrate; 1 g Dietary Fibre

Paré Pointer
A squirrel's nest is better known as the nutcracker suite.

Salads

Warm Pork And Apple Salad

A vibrant salad in both appearance and taste! Bright and colourful with red cabbage. Makes a large salad that could feed a hungry crowd. Shred cabbage and chop apple, green onion and almonds while tenderloin is searing.

Pork tenderloin	1 lb.	454 g
Cooking oil	1 tsp.	5 mL
MAPLE VINAIGRETTE		
Olive (or cooking) oil	1/3 cup	75 mL
Apple cider vinegar	3 tbsp.	50 mL
Maple syrup	3 tbsp.	50 mL
Grainy mustard	2 tbsp.	30 mL
Salt	1/4 tsp.	1 mL
Pepper	1/4 tsp.	1 mL
Shredded red cabbage	10 cups	2.5 L
Chopped tart cooking apple (such as Granny Smith), with peel	2 1/2 cups	625 mL
Chopped green onion	1 1/2 cups	375 mL
Coarsely chopped smoked almonds	3/4 cup	175 mL

Sear pork in cooking oil in large frying pan on medium for about 15 minutes until well browned on all sides. Remove to plate. Cover. Let stand for 5 minutes.

Maple Vinaigrette: While pork is searing, combine first 6 ingredients in jar with tight-fitting lid. Shake well. Makes 3/4 cup (175 mL) vinaigrette.

Cut pork into 1/4 inch (6 mm) thick slices. Transfer to large serving bowl. Add next 4 ingredients. Stir. Drizzle vinaigrette over salad. Toss. Makes 16 cups (4 L).

1 cup (250 mL): 152 Calories; 10.3 g Total Fat; 78 mg Sodium; 8 g Protein; 9 g Carbohydrate; 1 g Dietary Fibre

Pictured on page 71.

Creamy Pink Dressing

Thick and creamy. Could also be used as a dip or sandwich sauce.
Similar to Thousand Island salad dressing.

Salad dressing (or mayonnaise)	1/2 cup	125 mL
Chili sauce (or ketchup)	1 tbsp.	15 mL
Dried chives	1 tsp.	5 mL
Sweet pickle relish	1 tsp.	5 mL
Paprika	1/4 tsp.	1 mL

Combine all 5 ingredients in small jar with tight-fitting lid. Shake well. Makes 1/2 cup (125 mL).

2 tbsp. (30 mL): 159 Calories; 14.7 g Total Fat; 253 mg Sodium; 1 g Protein; 6 g Carbohydrate; trace Dietary Fibre

Hot Bacon Dressing

Delicious on fresh spinach leaves and sliced mushrooms.
Can be refrigerated for up to 3 days and reheated.

Bacon slices, diced	3	3
All-purpose flour	2 tbsp.	30 mL
Water	1 cup	250 mL
White vinegar	1/4 cup	60 mL
Granulated sugar	2 tbsp.	30 mL

Fry bacon in frying pan for about 4 minutes until crisp. Do not drain.

Sprinkle flour over bacon. Mix well. Add water. Heat and stir until boiling and thickened.

Add vinegar and sugar. Stir to dissolve sugar. Makes 1 1/4 cups (300 mL).

2 tbsp. (30 mL): 45 Calories; 2.9 g Total Fat; 41 mg Sodium; 1 g Protein; 4 g Carbohydrate; trace Dietary Fibre

Coconut Shrimp Soup

This Thai-influenced soup is sure to warm you up inside.
Alter green curry paste to suit your taste for heat.

Finely grated gingerroot (or 1/2 tsp., 2 mL, ground ginger)	2 tsp.	10 mL
Garlic cloves, minced (or 1/2 tsp., 2 mL, powder)	2	2
Green curry paste	1 tbsp.	15 mL
Cooking oil	2 tsp.	10 mL
Cans of light coconut milk (14 oz., 398 mL, each)	2	2
Prepared chicken broth	1 cup	250 mL
Stalk of lemon grass, halved	1	1
Fish sauce	2 tsp.	10 mL
Brown sugar, packed	2 tsp.	10 mL
Fresh pea pods, thinly sliced lengthwise	4 oz.	113 g
Raw medium shrimp, peeled and deveined	1 lb.	454 g
Fresh sweet basil (or 2 1/4 tsp., 11 mL, dried)	3 tbsp.	50 mL
Fresh cilantro (or parsley)	3 tbsp.	50 mL

Sauté ginger, garlic and curry paste in cooking oil in large saucepan for 1 to 2 minutes until fragrant.

Add next 6 ingredients. Stir. Bring to a boil on medium-high. Cover. Reduce heat to medium. Simmer for 2 minutes to blend flavours.

Add remaining 3 ingredients. Reduce heat to medium-low. Heat and stir for 3 to 5 minutes until shrimp are just pink. Remove and discard lemon grass. Makes 6 cups (1.5 L).

1 cup (250 mL): 254 Calories; 15.9 g Total Fat; 384 mg Sodium; 20 g Protein; 9 g Carbohydrate; trace Dietary Fibre

Pictured on page 72.

Soups

Black Bean Corn Soup

A Southwestern-style soup that has a bite to the otherwise corn-sweet base. Just the right thickness to pair with a biscuit. Add a salad to complete this quick meatless meal. Dice red onion and grate cheese while soup is simmering.

Chopped onion	1/2 cup	125 mL
Hard margarine (or butter)	2 tsp.	10 mL
Can of black beans, drained and rinsed	19 oz.	540 mL
Prepared chicken broth	1 3/4 cups	425 mL
Can of cream-style corn	14 oz.	398 mL
Chili sauce	1/2 cup	125 mL
Finely diced red onion	1/4 cup	60 mL
Grated sharp Cheddar cheese	1/4 cup	60 mL

Sauté onion in margarine in large saucepan for about 4 minutes until soft.

Add next 4 ingredients. Stir. Bring to a boil on medium-high. Reduce heat to medium-low. Simmer, uncovered, for 15 minutes, stirring frequently, to blend flavours.

Sprinkle individual servings with red onion and cheese. Makes 6 cups (1.5 L).

1 cup (250 mL): 187 Calories; 4 g Total Fat; 917 mg Sodium; 9 g Protein; 32 g Carbohydrate; 5 g Dietary Fibre

1. Bacon And Sun-Dried Tomato Sandwiches, page 24
2. Tomato Cheese Sandwich, page 25
3. Shrimp And Asparagus Wraps, page 30

Celery Chowder

Similar to commercial product—but even better! A hearty rich soup that is easy to make. Great alternative to corn or clam chowder. Serve with Chicken And Stuffing Quesadillas, page 83, for a filling meal.

Chopped onion	1/2 cup	125 mL
Finely diced celery	2 cups	500 mL
Medium potatoes, diced	2	2
Water	2 cups	500 mL
Milk	3 cups	750 mL
Salt	1 1/2 tsp.	7 mL
Pepper	1/8 tsp.	0.5 mL
Ground thyme, sprinkle		
Parsley flakes	1/2 tsp.	2 mL
Milk	1/4 cup	60 mL
All-purpose flour	1/4 cup	60 mL

Cook onion, celery and potato in water in large saucepan on medium-high for about 10 minutes until potato is tender.

Stir in first amount of milk. Add salt, pepper, thyme and parsley. Bring to a boil, stirring often.

Stir second amount of milk into flour in small bowl until smooth. Stir into milk mixture. Heat and stir until boiling and thickened. Makes 6 cups (1.5 L).

1 cup (250 mL): 121 Calories; 1.7 g Total Fat; 703 mg Sodium; 6 g Protein; 20 g Carbohydrate; 2 g Dietary Fibre

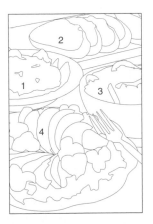

1. Pickled Beet Salad, page 42
2. Pesto Parmesan Toasts, page 34
3. Seafood Salad, page 46
4. Fresh Fruit Salad, page 44

Props Courtesy Of: Pfaltzgraff Canada

Rice Vegetable Beef Soup

A beef-flavoured broth soup with a mixture of vegetables and rice.
Celery is still tender-crisp. Use leftover roast beef in this tasty soup. Prepare the
vegetables while the water and bouillon cubes are coming to a boil.

Water	7 cups	1.75 L
Beef bouillon cubes	4	4
Grated carrot	1 1/2 cups	375 mL
Chopped zucchini, with peel	1 cup	250 mL
Thinly sliced celery	1/2 cup	125 mL
Minced onion flakes	1 tbsp.	15 mL
Pepper, just a pinch		
Ketchup	2 tbsp.	30 mL
Chopped cooked roast beef	2/3 cup	150 mL
Cooked long grain white (or brown) rice	1 cup	250 mL
Chopped fresh parsley (or 1 tbsp., 15 mL, flakes)	1/4 cup	60 mL

Combine water and bouillon cubes in large saucepan. Bring to a boil on medium-high.

Add next 7 ingredients. Stir. Bring to a boil. Reduce heat to medium. Cover. Simmer, stirring occasionally, for about 20 minutes until vegetables are tender.

Add rice. Stir. Cover. Simmer for 10 minutes.

Sprinkle parsley over vegetable mixture. Stir. Makes about 9 cups (2.25 L).

1 cup (250 mL): 125 Calories; 1.3 g Total Fat; 692 mg Sodium; 6 g Protein; 22 g Carbohydrate;
1 g Dietary Fibre

 To have extra cooked rice or pasta on hand, double or triple the recipe the next time you make it. Cool the extra amount. Put 1 cup (250 mL) servings into resealable freezer bags. Squeeze out the air. Seal. Freeze. Reheat in the microwave for on-the-go meals such as stir-fries or side dishes.

Tomato Chick Pea Soup

A very colourful soup with extraordinary fresh lemon zest flavour.
If desired, use a hotter curry paste to spice things up. Top with dollops
of plain yogurt. Ideal with a fresh loaf of crusty bread or buns!

Medium onion, chopped	1	1
Garlic cloves, minced (or 1 tsp., 5 mL, powder)	4	4
Cooking oil	1 tbsp.	15 mL
Mild curry paste	3 tbsp.	50 mL
Can of diced tomatoes	28 oz.	796 mL
Prepared vegetable (or chicken) broth	2 cups	500 mL
Tomato paste	3 tbsp.	50 mL
Granulated sugar	1 tsp.	5 mL
Can of chick peas (garbanzo beans), drained and rinsed	19 oz.	540 mL
Spinach leaves, stems removed	3 cups	750 mL
Salt, to taste		
Finely grated lemon zest	1 tsp.	5 mL

Sauté onion and garlic in cooking oil in large pot or Dutch oven for about 5 minutes until onion is soft.

Add curry paste. Heat and stir for 1 minute until fragrant.

Add next 4 ingredients. Bring to a boil on medium-high.

Add chick peas, spinach and salt. Heat and stir for about 3 minutes until heated through.

Add lemon zest. Stir. Makes 8 cups (2 L).

1 cup (250 mL): 135 Calories; 5.2 g Total Fat; 464 mg Sodium; 6 g Protein; 18 g Carbohydrate; 4 g Dietary Fibre

Pictured on page 71.

Cauliflower Cream Soup

Nice taste of cauliflower. Creamy texture. Buttered bread crumbs
are a nice touch. Serve with biscuits or a sandwich.

Hard margarine (or butter)	1 tbsp.	15 mL
Fine dry bread crumbs	1/4 cup	60 mL
Medium head of cauliflower (or 4 cups, 1 L, frozen)	1	1
Prepared chicken broth	2 cups	500 mL
Hard margarine (or butter)	3 tbsp.	50 mL
All-purpose flour	3 tbsp.	50 mL
Salt	1/4 tsp.	1 mL
Pepper	1/8 tsp.	0.5 mL
Prepared chicken broth	2 cups	500 mL
Half-and-half cream	1/4 cup	60 mL
Egg yolks (large)	2	2

Melt first amount of margarine in microwave-safe dish on high (100%). Stir in bread crumbs until well mixed. Set aside.

Cut cauliflower into 1 inch (2.5 cm) pieces. Simmer, uncovered, in first amount of chicken broth in large saucepan until tender-crisp. Do not drain. Transfer cauliflower and liquid to blender. Process until smooth.

While cauliflower is cooking, melt second amount of margarine in small saucepan. Stir in flour, salt and pepper until smooth. Slowly stir in second amount of chicken broth. Heat and stir on medium-high until boiling and slightly thickened. Add cauliflower mixture. Stir.

Whisk cream and egg yolks together in small bowl. Stir into cauliflower mixture. Sprinkle bread crumb mixture over individual servings of soup. Makes about 6 1/2 cups (1.6 L).

1 cup (250 mL): 166 Calories; 11 g Total Fat; 743 mg Sodium; 7 g Protein; 11 g Carbohydrate; 1 g Dietary Fibre

Potato Noodle Soup

Hearty and filling. Creamy and thick.

Large onion, finely chopped	1	1
Hard margarine (or butter)	1 tbsp.	15 mL
Box of scalloped potatoes, with seasoning	5 1/2 oz.	149 g
Water	6 1/2 cups	1.6 L
Dried vegetable flakes	1/2 cup	125 mL
Chicken bouillon powder	1 tbsp.	15 mL
Worcestershire sauce	1 tbsp.	15 mL
Package of instant noodles with chicken-flavoured packet, broken up and seasoning packet reserved	3 oz.	85 g
Milk (or half-and-half cream)	1 cup	250 mL
All-purpose flour	3 tbsp.	50 mL

Sauté onion in margarine in large saucepan on medium until beginning to brown.

While onion is sautéing, break up potatoes. Add potatoes and seasoning to onion mixture. Add next 4 ingredients. Bring to a boil on medium-high. Reduce heat to medium-low. Cover. Simmer for 15 minutes until potato is soft.

Stir in noodles and seasoning packet. Cover. Simmer for 5 minutes.

Stir milk into flour in small bowl until smooth. Stir into noodle mixture until boiling and slightly thickened. Makes 8 cups (2 L).

1 cup (250 mL): 289 Calories; 12.1 g Total Fat; 1667 mg Sodium; 7 g Protein; 40 g Carbohydrate; 2 g Dietary Fibre

Paré Pointer
Little Johnny didn't lose his two front teeth.
He has them in his pocket.

Egg Drop Soup

Threads of white contrast nicely with the dark broth.
Prepare the spinach, green onions and basil leaves while
the broth mixture is heating. Use leftover diced chicken.
Serve with biscuits or a sandwich.

Cans of condensed chicken broth (10 oz., 284 mL, each)	2	2
Water	4 cups	1 L
Indonesian sweet (or thick) soy sauce	1 tbsp.	15 mL
Chili sauce	3 tbsp.	50 mL
Dried crushed chilies	1/4 tsp.	1 mL
Garlic clove, minced (or 1/4 tsp., 1 mL, powder), optional	1	1
Large eggs, fork-beaten	2	2
Diced cooked chicken	2/3 cup	150 mL
Fresh spinach leaves, stems removed, lightly packed, cut chiffonade (see Note)	1 cup	250 mL
Green onions, thinly cut on diagonal	2	2
Lemon juice (or to taste)	2 tsp.	10 mL
Fresh bean sprouts (about 2 1/2 oz., 70 g)	1 cup	250 mL
Chopped fresh sweet basil (or mint) leaves (optional)	1 tbsp.	15 mL

Mix first 6 ingredients in large saucepan. Bring to a boil on medium-high.

Reduce heat to medium-low. Swirl broth mixture with fork, while slowly pouring egg into centre of whirlpool until fine threads form.

Add chicken, spinach and green onion. Cook, uncovered, for 3 minutes until heated through.

Stir in lemon juice.

Put bean sprouts and basil into individual bowls. Ladle in broth mixture. Makes 7 cups (1.75 L).

1 cup (250 mL): 92 Calories; 3.5 g Total Fat; 748 mg Sodium; 11 g Protein; 4 g Carbohydrate; 1 g Dietary Fibre

Note: To cut chiffonade, stack a few leaves at a time and roll up tightly. Slice crosswise into very thin strips.

Sautéed Spinach With Apricots

*Nice mix of colour, texture and flavour. An interesting twist on spinach.
Sunflower seeds add a bit of crunch while the sauce has subtle notes of
cumin in the background. Great with Sole Salmon Rolls, page 100.*

Garlic cloves, minced (or 1/2 tsp., 2 mL, powder)	2	2
Ground cumin	1/2 tsp.	2 mL
Hard margarine (or butter)	2 tbsp.	30 mL
Dried apricots, finely chopped	1/3 cup	75 mL
White (or alcohol-free) wine	1/3 cup	75 mL
Whipping cream	1/2 cup	125 mL
Salt	1/4 tsp.	1 mL
Pepper	1/4 tsp.	1 mL
Bag of fresh spinach leaves, stems removed	10 oz.	300 g
Roasted sunflower seeds	1/4 cup	60 mL

Sauté garlic and cumin in margarine in large frying pan for 1 minute until
fragrant.

Add apricots and wine. Heat and stir for about 3 minutes until most liquid
is evaporated.

Add whipping cream, salt and pepper. Simmer, uncovered, on medium for
3 minutes, stirring occasionally, to blend flavours.

Add spinach. Heat and stir for about 3 minutes until spinach is just wilted.

Add sunflower seeds. Stir. Makes about 2 cups (500 mL).

*1/2 cup (125 mL): 258 Calories; 20.5 g Total Fat; 290 mg Sodium; 5 g Protein; 14 g Carbohydrate;
4 g Dietary Fibre*

Pictured on page 90.

Saucy Carrot Fry

Lots of creamy, thick sauce. Smoky bacon and peppery undertones.

Milk	1 cup	250 mL
Cornstarch	2 tsp.	10 mL
Green onion, sliced	1	1
Salt	1/4 tsp.	1 mL
Pepper	1/4 tsp.	1 mL
Bacon slices, diced	4	4
Medium carrots (about 1 1/2 lbs., 680 g), cut into thin diagonal slices (about 4 cups, 1 L)	7	7
Shoestring potato chips (original flavour), for garnish	1 cup	250 mL

Stir first 5 ingredients together in small bowl. Set aside.

Fry bacon in hot wok or frying pan for 2 minutes until starting to cook.

Add carrot. Stir-fry for 6 to 7 minutes until tender-crisp. Stir milk mixture. Add to carrot mixture. Heat and stir until boiling and slightly thickened.

Turn into serving dish. Sprinkle potato sticks over carrot mixture. Serves 4.

1 serving: 208 Calories; 11.1 g Total Fat; 382 mg Sodium; 6 g Protein; 22 g Carbohydrate; 4 g Dietary Fibre

Hot Dilled Carrots

These glisten in the dish. Very tasty and very easy.

Sliced carrot (about 1/4 inch, 6 mm, thick)	4 cups	1 L
Water	1/2 tsp.	2 mL
Hard margarine (or butter)	2 tbsp.	30 mL
Chopped fresh dill (or 1/2 tsp., 2 mL, dill weed)	2 tsp.	10 mL
Salt, sprinkle		
Pepper, sprinkle		

(continued on next page)

Cook carrot in water in large saucepan for 6 to 8 minutes until tender. Drain.

Add margarine and dill. Toss to coat. Add salt and pepper. Makes 4 cups (1 L).

1/2 cup (125 mL): 63 Calories; 3 g Total Fat; 88 mg Sodium; 1 g Protein; 9 g Carbohydrate; 2 g Dietary Fibre

Pictured on page 89.

Orange Couscous And Green Beans

Delicate flavour of orange. Looks so appetizing. Goes great with pork or poultry. Wonderful with Sweet And Sour Turkey, page 94.

Prepared chicken broth	2 cups	500 mL
Couscous	2 cups	500 mL
Olive (or cooking) oil	2 tbsp.	30 mL
Green beans	9 oz.	255 g
Water		
Finely grated orange peel	2 tsp.	10 mL
Brown sugar, packed	2 tsp.	10 mL
Salt	1/4 tsp.	1 mL
Pepper	1/4 tsp.	1 mL
Hard margarine (or butter)	2 tsp.	10 mL

Bring broth to a boil in large saucepan. Remove from heat. Add couscous and olive oil. Stir. Cover. Let stand for 5 minutes.

Trim beans. Cut in half. Cook in water in separate large saucepan on medium for about 5 minutes until tender-crisp. Drain.

Fluff couscous mixture with fork. Add next 4 ingredients. Stir.

Add beans and margarine. Stir. Makes 6 cups (1.5 L).

1/2 cup (125 mL): 165 Calories; 3.4 g Total Fat; 198 mg Sodium; 5 g Protein; 28 g Carbohydrate; 2 g Dietary Fibre

Pictured on page 89.

Glazed Parsnips

Parsnips and orange complement each other well.
Sweet citrus notes with a slight tang. Excellent!

Parsnips, cut bite size (about 8 cups, 2 L)	2 lbs.	900 g
Water		
Salt	1/2 tsp.	2 mL
Hard margarine (or butter)	2 tbsp.	30 mL
Orange marmalade	1/3 cup	75 mL

Cook parsnip in water and salt in large saucepan for 6 to 8 minutes until tender. Drain.

While parsnip is cooking, melt margarine in small saucepan. Add marmalade. Stir. Pour over cooked parsnips. Stir gently until coated. Serves 6 to 8.

1 serving: 176 Calories; 4.2 g Total Fat; 68 mg Sodium; 2 g Protein; 35 g Carbohydrate;
4 g Dietary Fibre

Sweet Potato With Basil

Subtle bacon flavour. Slight sweetness with the basil. Will become a family favourite. Nice change to have sweet potatoes instead of regular potatoes. Serve with Dilled Fish, page 106.

Cubed sweet potato	4 cups	1 L
Water		
Salt	1 tsp.	5 mL
Green onions	4	4
Hard margarine (or butter)	2 tbsp.	30 mL
Honey Dijon mustard	2 tbsp.	30 mL
Chopped fresh sweet basil	2 tbsp.	30 mL
Pre-packaged cooked, crumbled bacon (about 6 slices), see Note	6 tbsp.	100 mL

(continued on next page)

Side Dishes

Cook sweet potato in water and salt in large saucepan for about 15 minutes until just tender. Drain well.

While sweet potato is cooking, chop green onions. Sauté in margarine in large frying pan for 3 to 5 minutes until soft.

Add mustard and basil. Stir. Add sweet potato. Toss.

Sprinkle bacon over sweet potato mixture. Makes 4 cups (1 L).

1/2 cup (125 mL): 132 Calories; 5.7 g Total Fat; 172 mg Sodium; 3 g Protein; 18 g Carbohydrate; 2 g Dietary Fibre

Pictured on page 126.

Note: If you would prefer to have your own crumbled bacon on hand, fry bacon slices until very crisp. Drain on paper towel. When cool, crumble and put into resealable freezer bag. 1 slice = 1 tbsp. (15 mL) crumbled.

Creamed Niblets

Creamy corn is crisp and sweet. A great way to dress up a can of corn. Serve with Wingin' It Wings, page 91.

Hard margarine (or butter)	2 tbsp.	30 mL
All-purpose flour	2 tbsp.	30 mL
Salt	1/4 tsp.	1 mL
Pepper, sprinkle		
Milk	1 cup	250 mL
Minced onion flakes (optional)	1 tsp.	5 mL
Chicken bouillon powder	1/2 tsp.	2 mL
Can of kernel corn, drained	12 oz.	341 mL

Melt margarine in medium saucepan. Stir in flour, salt and pepper until smooth. Stir in milk until boiling and thickened.

Add onion flakes, bouillon and corn. Stir. Bring to a boil. Reduce heat. Simmer, uncovered, until heated through. Makes 2 cups (500 mL). Serves 4.

1 serving: 154 Calories; 7 g Total Fat; 536 mg Sodium; 4 g Protein; 21 g Carbohydrate; 2 g Dietary Fibre

Quickest Mashed Potatoes

These may be the quickest mashed potatoes you'll ever make!
Firm, smooth texture. Serve with Creamed Pork Chops, page 119.

Light cream cheese, cut up	2 oz.	62 g
Hard margarine (or butter)	2 tbsp.	30 mL
Milk	1 cup	250 mL
Water	1 cup	250 mL
Onion salt	1 1/2 tsp.	7 mL
Pepper	1/8 tsp.	0.5 mL
Instant potato flakes	2 cups	500 mL
Chopped fresh dill (or 1/2 tsp., 2 mL, dill weed)	2 tsp.	10 mL

Combine first 6 ingredients in large saucepan. Heat on medium, stirring often, until cream cheese is melted and mixture is very hot.

Add potato flakes. Stir well. Sprinkle dill over potato mixture. Makes 2 3/4 cups (675 mL).

1/2 cup (125 mL): 143 Calories; 6.8 g Total Fat; 487 mg Sodium; 4 g Protein; 17 g Carbohydrate; 1 g Dietary Fibre

Sesame Broccoli

Pleasant soy flavour complements the broccoli. Sesame seeds evenly dispersed.

Fresh (or frozen) broccoli, cut up (about 4 cups, 1 L)	1 lb.	454 g
Water		
Hard margarine (or butter)	1 tbsp.	15 mL
Soy sauce	1 tbsp.	15 mL
White vinegar	2 tsp.	10 mL
Toasted sesame seeds (see Note)	1 tbsp.	15 mL
Granulated sugar	2 tsp.	10 mL

Cook broccoli in water in large saucepan for about 4 minutes until tender-crisp. Drain.

(continued on next page)

Side Dishes

While broccoli is cooking, mix remaining 5 ingredients in small cup. Microwave on high (100%) for about 1 1/2 minutes until boiling and slightly thickened. Drizzle over broccoli. Toss until well coated. Serves 4.

1 serving: 77 Calories; 4.4 g Total Fat; 321 mg Sodium; 4 g Protein; 8 g Carbohydrate; 3 g Dietary Fibre

Pictured on page 89.

Note: Packages of pre-toasted sesame seeds are often available in produce sections of grocery stores.

Beans With Onion

Flavours come together deliciously. Vinegar tang but with a nutty, slightly smoky flavour. Tasty with Pineapple Steak, page 142.

Bacon slice, diced	1	1
Chopped onion	1/4 cup	60 mL
Can of cut green beans, drained (or 2 cups, 500 mL, fresh or frozen, cooked)	14 oz.	398 mL
Red wine (or balsamic) vinegar	2 tsp.	10 mL
Salt	1/8 tsp.	0.5 mL
Pepper	1/8 tsp.	0.5 mL
Coarsely chopped salted peanuts	2 tbsp.	30 mL

Sauté bacon and onion in medium saucepan on medium-high for 3 to 5 minutes until browned. Reduce heat to medium.

Stir in beans, vinegar, salt and pepper. Cover. Cook for 3 to 4 minutes until heated through.

Sprinkle peanuts over bean mixture. Stir. Serves 4.

1 serving: 74 Calories; 4.9 g Total Fat; 367 mg Sodium; 3 g Protein; 6 g Carbohydrate; 2 g Dietary Fibre

Pictured on page 126.

Beef And Sprouts

*Fresh vegetables add wonderful flavour, a crunchy texture
and a bit of colour to this enjoyable dish. Easy and fast.*

Lean ground beef	1 lb.	454 g
Medium onion, chopped	1	1
Thinly sliced celery	1/2 cup	125 mL
Fresh pea pods	1 cup	250 mL
Water	3/4 cup	175 mL
Beef bouillon powder	1 tbsp.	15 mL
Fresh bean sprouts	2 cups	500 mL
Soy sauce	4 tsp.	20 mL
Water	2 tbsp.	30 mL
Cornstarch	4 tsp.	20 mL

Scramble-fry ground beef, onion, celery and pea pods in large frying pan
on medium-high until beef starts to brown and vegetables are tender-crisp.

Add first amount of water, bouillon powder, bean sprouts and soy sauce.
Stir.

Stir second amount of water into cornstarch in small cup until smooth. Stir
into beef mixture. Heat and stir until boiling and slightly thickened. Makes
4 1/4 cups (1 L). Serves 4.

*1 serving: 311 Calories; 17.6 g Total Fat; 888 mg Sodium; 25 g Protein; 13 g Carbohydrate;
2 g Dietary Fibre*

Pictured on page 107.

Paré Pointer

*Junk is what you've kept for many years and throw away
just before you need it.*

Main Dishes

Steak In Gravy

Enjoy this tender meat in a rich and tasty gravy cooked in the pressure cooker.
Serve with noodles or mashed potatoes prepared while the steak is cooking.

Round steak, cut into 6 serving-size pieces	1 1/2 lbs.	680 g
Cooking oil	1 tbsp.	15 mL
Water	2 cups	500 mL
All-purpose flour	3 tbsp.	50 mL
Beef bouillon powder	2 tsp.	10 mL
Salt	1/2 tsp.	2 mL
Pepper	1/4 tsp.	1 mL
Medium onion, chopped	1	1
Sliced fresh mushrooms	1 1/2 cups	375 mL

Brown both sides of steak in cooking oil in pressure cooker. Transfer to plate. Keep warm.

Gradually stir water into flour in medium bowl until smooth. Add bouillon powder, salt and pepper. Stir. Pour into pressure cooker. Heat and stir until boiling and thickened. Place rack in pressure cooker. Place steak on rack.

Add onion and mushrooms. Lock lid in place. Bring pressure cooker up to pressure on high. Reduce heat to medium-low just to maintain even pressure. Cook for 15 minutes. Remove from heat. Allow pressure to drop naturally. Remove lid. Serves 6.

1 serving: 201 Calories; 7.3 g Total Fat; 458 mg Sodium; 27 g Protein; 6 g Carbohydrate; 1 g Dietary Fibre

 Deliberately plan to have leftovers that can either be reheated in the microwave for a really quick supper, or used in another recipe on a rushed day to reduce preparation time. (See Plan-Ahead Dishes, pages 134 to 139.)

Sun-Dried Tomato Butter Steaks

Double the flavoured butter to have extra for an even quicker supper the next time.

SUN-DRIED TOMATO BUTTER

Butter (not margarine), softened	1/3 cup	75 mL
Freshly grated Parmesan cheese	1/4 cup	60 mL
Chopped fresh sweet basil	3 tbsp.	50 mL
Sun-dried tomato pesto	2 tbsp.	30 mL
Pepper	1/2 tsp.	2 mL
Garlic salt	1/4 tsp.	1 mL
Sun-dried tomato pesto	3 tbsp.	50 mL
T-bone steaks (about 2 3/4 lbs., 1.25 kg)	4	4

Sun-Dried Tomato Butter: Preheat barbecue to medium-high. While barbecue is heating, combine first 6 ingredients in small bowl. Spread on waxed paper to 4 inch (10 cm) disk. Cover. Freeze for 15 minutes until firm.

While butter is chilling, spread second amount of pesto on both sides of each steak. Cook on greased grill over medium-high heat for 5 to 10 minutes per side until desired doneness. Cut flavoured butter disk into 4 wedges. Place 1 wedge on each steak. Serves 4.

1 serving: 832 Calories; 60.2 g Total Fat; 520 mg Sodium; 67 g Protein; 3 g Carbohydrate; trace Dietary Fibre

1. Warm Pork And Apple Salad, page 49
2. Tomato Chick Pea Soup, page 57
3. Crab Filling, page 26

Main Dishes

Winter Steak

This tender steak is for onion and garlic lovers. The tea is subtle, but there.

Water	1/2 cup	125 mL
Orange pekoe tea bags	2	2
Top sirloin steaks (about 1 1/2 lbs., 680 g)	6	6
Hard margarine (or butter)	4 tsp.	20 mL
Large onion, cut into rings	1	1
Garlic cloves, minced (or 1 tsp., 5 mL, powder)	4	4

Bring water to a boil in small saucepan. Add tea bags. Remove from heat. Steep for 10 minutes.

While tea is steeping, sear steak in margarine in large frying pan on medium-high for 30 seconds per side. Reduce heat to medium. Brown for 7 to 9 minutes per side until desired doneness. Remove steak to plate, leaving drippings in frying pan. Tent steak with foil to keep warm.

Add onion and garlic to drippings. Sauté for 4 minutes, stirring constantly, until starting to brown. Add tea to onion mixture. Boil, uncovered, for 4 minutes until onion is soft and liquid is absorbed. Spoon onion mixture over each steak. Serves 6.

1 serving: 219 Calories; 12.7 g Total Fat; 95 mg Sodium; 22 g Protein; 3 g Carbohydrate; trace Dietary Fibre

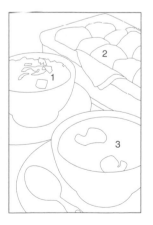

1. Meatless Chili, page 111
2. Crusty Cheese Biscuits, page 38
3. Coconut Shrimp Soup, page 51

Swiss Steak

Tomato, beefy flavour. Economy meat made tender in the pressure cooker.

All-purpose flour	1/4 cup	60 mL
Paprika	1 tsp.	5 mL
Seasoned salt	1 tsp.	5 mL
Pepper	1/2 tsp.	2 mL
Beef round steak (1/2 inch, 12 mm, thick), cut into 8 serving-size pieces	2 lbs.	900 g
Cooking oil	1 tbsp.	15 mL
Prepared horseradish	1 tbsp.	15 mL
Can of diced tomatoes, with juice	14 oz.	398 mL
Granulated sugar	1 tsp.	5 mL
Baby carrots	24	24
Sliced celery	1/2 cup	125 mL
Large onion, cut lengthwise into 8 wedges	1	1

Mix first 4 ingredients in small shallow dish or on waxed paper. Press steak into flour mixture to coat completely.

Heat 1 1/2 tsp. (7 mL) cooking oil in pressure cooker on medium. Brown steak, in 2 batches, on both sides, adding remaining cooking oil for second batch. Return steak to pressure cooker.

Meanwhile, stir horseradish, tomatoes and sugar together in small bowl. Pour over browned steak.

Layer carrots, celery and onion on steak. Lock lid in place. Bring pressure cooker up to pressure on medium-high. Reduce heat to medium just to maintain even pressure. Cook for 15 minutes. Remove from heat. Allow pressure to drop naturally. Remove lid. Serves 8.

1 serving: 221 Calories; 6.8 g Total Fat; 315 mg Sodium; 27 g Protein; 12 g Carbohydrate; 2 g Dietary Fibre

Variation: Remove vegetables and meat with slotted spoon to shallow casserole. Stir 1/3 cup (75 mL) water into 2 tbsp. (30 mL) flour in small dish until smooth. Add to juices in pressure cooker. Heat and stir on medium until boiling and thickened. Makes about 1 2/3 cups (400 mL) gravy. Pour over steak and vegetables.

Skillet Supper

An express form of beef stew! Kids will like this. Simple, slightly sweet, creamy corn taste. Trick to cooking in a short amount of time is to cut vegetables small.

Lean ground beef	1 lb.	454 g
Medium onion, chopped	1	1
Diced potato	3 cups	750 mL
Medium carrots, thinly sliced diagonally	3	3
Can of condensed beef consommé	10 oz.	284 mL
Can of cream-style corn	14 oz.	398 mL
Frozen peas (optional)	1 cup	250 mL
Salt	1 tsp.	5 mL
Pepper	1/4 tsp.	1 mL

Scramble-fry ground beef and onion in large non-stick frying pan on medium-high until onion is soft and beef is no longer pink. Drain.

Stir in potato, carrot and consommé. Bring to a boil. Reduce heat to medium. Cover. Simmer for about 15 minutes until potato and carrot are tender.

Add corn, peas, salt and pepper. Heat and stir until heated through. Makes 6 cups (1.5 L). Serves 4.

1 serving: 400 Calories; 10.5 g Total Fat; 1371 mg Sodium; 29 g Protein; 51 g Carbohydrate; 5 g Dietary Fibre

Pictured on page 108.

 To store ground beef in recipe-size portions, buy in bulk (not frozen) then separate into 1 lb. (454 g), 1 1/2 lb. (680 g) or 2 lb. (900 g) portions. Wrap in plastic wrap and place in resealable freezer bags. Label with weight. Freeze for up to 6 months.

Chung Beef Noodles

Tender-crisp vegetables and tender beef strips on a bed of saucy noodles.
Lots of flavour in the beef.

Liquid gravy browner (or water)	1 tbsp.	15 mL
Granulated sugar	2 tsp.	10 mL
Ground ginger	3/4 tsp.	4 mL
Seasoned salt	1/2 tsp.	2 mL
Top sirloin steak, cut into thin slivers	3/4 lb.	340 g
Water	1 1/2 cups	375 mL
Reserved seasoning packets	2	2
Packages of instant noodles with beef-flavoured packet (3 oz., 85 g, each), broken up, seasoning packets reserved	2	2
Frozen cut green beans	2 cups	500 mL
Can of sliced water chestnuts, drained	8 oz.	227 mL
Can of bamboo shoots, drained	8 oz.	227 mL
Sherry (or alcohol-free sherry), optional	1/4 cup	60 mL
Soy sauce	2 tbsp.	30 mL
Cooking oil	1 tbsp.	15 mL
Toasted sesame seeds (see Tip, page 42), sprinkle		

Mix gravy browner, sugar, ginger and seasoned salt in medium bowl. Add beef. Stir until well coated. Set aside.

Add water to wok or large frying pan. Bring to a boil. Add reserved seasoning packets. Stir to dissolve. Add noodles. Add next 5 ingredients. Stir. Bring to a boil. Reduce heat. Cover. Simmer for 3 minutes. Transfer to serving platter. Cover. Keep warm.

Heat cooking oil in same wok on medium-high until hot. Add beef mixture. Stir-fry until no pink remains. Spoon over noodle mixture.

Sprinkle sesame seeds over beef mixture. Makes 7 cups (1.75 L). Serves 4.

1 serving: 413 Calories; 13.5 g Total Fat; 1159 mg Sodium; 26 g Protein; 47 g Carbohydrate; 2 g Dietary Fibre

Variation: Omit green beans. Add 14 oz. (398 mL) can of baby corn, drained.

Main Dishes

Noodle Power

Power to make you want more. Hearty and filling. Thick and creamy.

Vermicelli	8 oz.	225 g
Boiling water	12 cups	3 L
Salt	2 tsp.	10 mL
Lean ground beef	1 lb.	454 g
Finely chopped onion	1/4 cup	60 mL
Chopped green pepper	1/2 cup	125 mL
Can of tomato sauce	7 1/2 oz.	213 mL
Block of light cream cheese, softened	8 oz.	250 g
Light creamed cottage cheese	1 cup	250 mL
Light sour cream	1/4 cup	60 mL
Seasoned salt	1/2 tsp.	2 mL
Pepper	1/4 tsp.	1 mL
Italian seasoning	1 tsp.	5 mL

Cook vermicelli in boiling water and salt in large uncovered pot or Dutch oven for 5 to 7 minutes until tender but firm. Drain. Return to pot.

Meanwhile, scramble-fry ground beef, onion and green pepper in large frying pan until beef is no longer pink.

Add tomato sauce. Stir.

Beat remaining 6 ingredients in medium bowl. Add to beef mixture. Add vermicelli. Heat and stir until bubbly. Makes 7 cups (1.75 L). Serves 4.

1 serving: 697 Calories; 31.6 g Total Fat; 1374 mg Sodium; 40 g Protein; 61 g Carbohydrate; 2 g Dietary Fibre

Paré Pointer

If you want some information about a fish, just drop him a line.

Stove-Top Taco Beef

Meaty, rich and spicy. Great for lunch or supper. Serve with a salad.

Frozen shredded hash brown potatoes	4 cups	1 L
Cooking oil	2 tsp.	10 mL
Medium green or red pepper	1	1
Medium onion	1	1
Medium carrots	2	2
Extra lean ground beef	1 lb.	454 g
Envelope of taco seasoning mix	1 1/4 oz.	35 g
Medium tomato, diced	1	1
Can of condensed tomato (or cream of mushroom) soup	10 oz.	284 mL
Water	1/2 cup	125 mL
Grated Monterey Jack With Jalapeño cheese	1 cup	250 mL

Fry potatoes in cooking oil in large non-stick frying pan for about 10 minutes, stirring occasionally, until soft and starting to brown.

While potatoes are cooking, chop green pepper and onion. Grate carrots.

Scramble-fry ground beef, green pepper, onion, carrot and seasoning mix in separate large frying pan for about 5 minutes until beef is no longer pink.

Stir in tomato, soup and water. Bring to a boil. Reduce heat to medium-low.

Spread potatoes over top. Scatter cheese over potatoes. Cook, uncovered, for about 15 minutes until bubbly and cheese is melted. Makes 7 cups (1.75 L). Serves 6.

1 serving: 479 Calories; 20.5 g Total Fat; 892 mg Sodium; 32 g Protein; 44 g Carbohydrate; 5 g Dietary Fibre

Main Dishes

Sweet And Sour Patties

*Great sized patties that are smothered with lots of rich brown
sauce and sautéed onion. Sauce is definitely
sweet and sour—lives up to its name!*

Medium onion, thinly sliced and separated into rings	1	1
Cooking oil	1 tbsp.	15 mL
PATTIES		
Milk	1/2 cup	125 mL
Fine dry bread crumbs	2/3 cup	150 mL
Seasoned salt	1/2 tsp.	2 mL
Onion salt	1/2 tsp.	2 mL
Pepper	1/4 tsp.	1 mL
Lean ground beef	1 lb.	454 g
SWEET AND SOUR SAUCE		
Brown sugar, packed	1 3/4 cups	425 mL
All-purpose flour	2 tbsp.	30 mL
Dry mustard	1/2 tsp.	2 mL
White vinegar	1/2 cup	125 mL
Water	1/3 cup	75 mL
Soy sauce	2 tbsp.	30 mL
Ketchup	1 tbsp.	15 mL

Sauté onion in cooking oil in medium frying pan until golden. Transfer to plate.

Patties: While onion is sautéing, stir next 5 ingredients in medium bowl.

Add ground beef. Mix well. Shape into 8 patties. Brown in same frying pan for 4 to 5 minutes per side until no longer pink inside.

Sweet And Sour Sauce: While patties are cooking, mix brown sugar, flour and mustard thoroughly in medium saucepan.

Stir in vinegar, water, soy sauce and ketchup. Heat and stir until boiling and thickened. Scatter onion over patties. Pour sauce over onion. Cover. Simmer for about 4 minutes until heated through. Serves 4.

1 serving: 788 Calories; 22.2 g Total Fat; 1160 mg Sodium; 26 g Protein; 124 g Carbohydrate; 2 g Dietary Fibre

Dinner Stew

*Full-bodied beef flavour with the addition of turnip cooked in
the pressure cooker. Just serve with some pickled beets.*

Worcestershire sauce	1 tsp.	5 mL
Salt	1 tsp.	5 mL
Pepper	1/4 tsp.	1 mL
Lemon juice	1 tsp.	5 mL
Granulated sugar	1/2 tsp.	2 mL
Garlic powder	1/8 tsp.	0.5 mL
Liquid gravy browner	1/4 tsp.	1 mL
Water	1 1/2 cups	375 mL
Beef stew meat	1 lb.	454 g
Cooking oil	1 tsp.	5 mL
Medium onion	1	1
Baby potatoes, with peel	8	8
Small yellow turnip	1	1
Baby carrots	12	12
Frozen peas	1 cup	250 mL
Water	1/4 cup	60 mL
Cornstarch	1 1/2 tbsp.	25 mL

Stir first 8 ingredients together in small bowl. Set aside.

Brown beef in cooking oil in pressure cooker on medium-high.

While beef is browning, cut onion into pieces, cut potatoes in half and
cube turnip. Add to browned beef. Add carrots. Pour water mixture over
vegetables. Stir. Lock lid in place. Bring pressure cooker up to pressure on
medium-high. Reduce heat to medium just to maintain even pressure.
Cook for 15 minutes. Remove from heat. Allow pressure to drop naturally.
Remove lid.

Stir in peas. Heat and stir on medium.

Stir water into cornstarch in small cup until smooth. Stir into stew. Heat
and stir until boiling and thickened. Makes about 6 cups (1.5 L). Serves 4.

*1 serving: 355 Calories; 11.3 g Total Fat; 774 mg Sodium; 30 g Protein; 33 g Carbohydrate;
5 g Dietary Fibre*

Chili Chicken

A pressure cooker recipe. Serve with guacamole, shredded lettuce, diced tomato, and cornbread or tortilla wedges. Add more dried crushed chilies for extra heat.

Chopped red onion	1 cup	250 mL
Thinly sliced celery	1 cup	250 mL
Chopped red pepper	1 cup	250 mL
Garlic cloves, minced (or 1 tsp., 5 mL, powder)	4	4
Cooking oil	1 tbsp.	15 mL
Ground chicken	1 lb.	454 g
Ground cumin	1 1/2 tbsp.	25 mL
Dried crushed chilies	2 tsp.	10 mL
Dried sweet basil	1 1/2 tbsp.	25 mL
Can of diced tomatoes, with juice	28 oz.	796 mL
Tomato paste	3 tbsp.	50 mL
Can of red kidney beans, rinsed and drained	19 oz.	540 mL
Salt, sprinkle		

Sauté red onion, celery, red pepper and garlic in cooking oil in pressure cooker on medium for about 5 minutes until onion is soft.

Add ground chicken. Scramble-fry for about 5 minutes until lightly browned.

Add next 5 ingredients. Stir. Lock lid in place. Bring pressure cooker up to pressure on high. Reduce heat to medium-low just to maintain even pressure. Cook for 10 minutes. Remove from heat. Allow pressure to drop naturally. Remove lid.

Add beans and salt. Stir. Heat through. Makes about 8 cups (2 L). Serves 4.

1 serving: 437 Calories; 20.7 g Total Fat; 607 mg Sodium; 30 g Protein; 37 g Carbohydrate; 9 g Dietary Fibre

Chicken And Mushroom Linguine

Flecks of green from the basil.
Generous amount of chicken. Yummy and creamy.

Lemon pepper (or plain) linguine pasta	8 oz.	225 g
Boiling water	8 cups	2 L
Salt	2 tsp.	10 mL
Boneless, skinless chicken breast halves (about 4), diced	1 lb.	454 g
Green onions, sliced diagonally	5	5
Sliced fresh mushrooms	2 cups	500 mL
Minced garlic (or 1/4 tsp., 1 mL, powder)	1 tsp.	5 mL
Olive (or cooking) oil	2 tbsp.	30 mL
Hard margarine (or butter)	3 tbsp.	50 mL
All-purpose flour	3 tbsp.	50 mL
Can of condensed chicken broth	10 oz.	284 mL
Homogenized milk	1 1/3 cups	325 mL
Chopped fresh sweet basil (or 1 1/2 tsp., 7 mL, dried)	2 tbsp.	30 mL
Finely grated Romano (or Parmesan) cheese	1/3 cup	75 mL

Cook pasta in boiling water and salt in large uncovered pot or Dutch oven for 8 to 10 minutes until tender but firm. Drain. Cover. Keep warm.

While pasta is cooking, sauté next 4 ingredients in olive oil in large frying pan for about 10 minutes until no pink remains in chicken. Add to pasta. Toss. Cover. Keep warm.

Melt margarine in same frying pan. Stir in flour until smooth. Heat and stir on medium for 30 seconds to cook slightly. Slowly stir in broth and milk until boiling and slightly thickened.

Stir in basil. Add sauce to pasta mixture. Sprinkle cheese over pasta mixture. Toss until well coated. Serve immediately. Makes 8 cups (2 L) pasta and sauce. Serves 4 to 6.

1 serving: 616 Calories; 24.6 g Total Fat; 728 mg Sodium; 43 g Protein; 54 g Carbohydrate; 2 g Dietary Fibre

Chicken And Stuffing Quesadillas

The flavour combination makes a great taste sensation. Soft in the middle and crunchy on the outside. You can skip cooking the chicken thighs and use leftover cooked chicken instead. Serve with Celery Chowder, page 55, for a filling supper.

Boneless, skinless chicken thighs (about 1/2 lb., 225 g), cut into 1/2 inch (12 mm) strips	4	4
Boiling water, to cover		
Salt	1/2 tsp.	2 mL
Box of stove-top stuffing mix	4 1/4 oz.	120 g
Green onions	3	3
Grated Monterey Jack cheese	1 1/2 cups	375 mL
Large flour tortillas (about 10 inches, 25 cm), see Tip, page 8	6	6

Cook chicken strips, uncovered, in boiling water and salt in small saucepan for about 8 minutes until tender. Drain. Dice strips. Makes 1 cup (250 mL).

While chicken is cooking, prepare stuffing mix according to package directions. Chop green onions.

Divide chicken, stuffing, green onion and cheese on 1/2 of each tortilla. Fold other 1/2 of each tortilla over filling. Brown both sides in large greased frying pan on medium for 2 minutes per side until cheese is melted. Makes 6 packets, each cutting into 4 wedges, for a total of 24 wedges.

1 wedge: 102 Calories; 3.8 g Total Fat; 203 mg Sodium; 5 g Protein; 11 g Carbohydrate; trace Dietary Fibre

 tip *When you have some extra time, cook (bake, poach or barbecue) a quantity of boneless, skinless chicken breast halves, seasoned with desired spices, marinade or barbecue sauce. Cool. Cover individually with plastic wrap. Place in resealable freezer bags. Freeze. Defrost as needed for use in salads, sandwiches or other dishes that call for cooked chicken.*

Chicken And Crab Casserole

A wonderful casserole that can be made in the microwave!
The chicken is tender and moist.

Cooking oil	1 tbsp.	15 mL
Medium leek (white and tender parts only), thinly sliced	1	1
Garlic cloves, minced (or 1/2 tsp., 2 mL, powder)	2	2
Bacon slices, chopped	4	4
Red baby potatoes	1 lb.	454 g
Prepared chicken broth	2/3 cup	150 mL
Boneless, skinless chicken thighs (about 12)	1 1/2 lbs.	680 g
Can of crabmeat, drained and cartilage removed, flaked	4 1/4 oz.	120 g
Water	1 tbsp.	15 mL
Cornstarch	2 tsp.	10 mL
Sour cream	1/3 cup	75 mL
Salt, sprinkle		
Pepper, sprinkle		

Combine first 4 ingredients in large microwave-safe dish. Cover. Microwave on high (100%) for 5 minutes, stirring twice during cooking, until leek is soft.

While leek and bacon are cooking, cut potatoes in half. Add to softened leek mixture. Add broth. Cover. Microwave on high (100%) for 10 minutes.

Meanwhile, quarter chicken thighs. Add to leek mixture. Stir. Cover. Microwave on high (100%) for about 10 minutes, stirring twice during cooking, until chicken is no longer pink.

Add crab. Mix well.

Stir water into cornstarch in small bowl until smooth. Stir into chicken mixture. Add sour cream, salt and pepper. Stir. Cover. Microwave on high (100%) for 3 to 4 minutes, stirring once during cooking, until mixture is thickened. Makes 4 cups (1 L).

1 cup (250 mL): 523 Calories; 26.3 g Total Fat; 513 mg Sodium; 44 g Protein; 26 g Carbohydrate; 3 g Dietary Fibre

 # Hazelnut Chicken

Thick coating on chicken. Definite hazelnut taste. Adds interest to fried chicken.

Boneless, skinless chicken breast halves (about 1 1/2 lbs., 680 g)	6	6
Large egg	1	1
Water	1 tbsp.	15 mL
Fine dry bread crumbs	1/2 cup	125 mL
Ground hazelnuts (filberts)	1/2 cup	125 mL
Salt	1 1/4 tsp.	6 mL
Pepper	1/2 tsp.	2 mL
Paprika	1 tsp.	5 mL
Cooking oil	2 tbsp.	30 mL

Place chicken between sheets of waxed paper. Pound with mallet or rolling pin until flat and thin.

Beat egg and water with fork in small bowl.

Stir next 5 ingredients together in separate shallow dish or on waxed paper. Dip chicken into egg mixture. Press into crumb mixture to coat completely.

Cook chicken in cooking oil in large frying pan on medium-high for 5 to 6 minutes per side until no longer pink. Remove to paper towels to drain. Serves 6.

1 serving: 282 Calories; 14.3 g Total Fat; 587 mg Sodium; 29 g Protein; 9 g Carbohydrate; 1 g Dietary Fibre

 Make up individual meal packages from leftovers and freeze in microwave-safe containers. Then, when you have "one of those days," simply pop a "TV" dinner into the microwave.

Chicken Parmesan

Tender, juicy chicken in a seasoned crumb coating. Nicely browned
with visible flecks of seasoning. Try the variation for a more
authentic rendition of this popular Italian dish.

Fine dry bread crumbs	3 tbsp.	50 mL
Chicken bouillon powder	1/4 tsp.	1 mL
Grated Parmesan cheese	3 tbsp.	50 mL
Ground oregano	1/2 tsp.	2 mL
Salt	1/2 tsp.	2 mL
Pepper	1/4 tsp.	1 mL
Boneless, skinless chicken breast halves (or thighs), about 1 lb. (454 g)	4	4
Cooking oil	2 tsp.	10 mL
Grated Parmesan cheese (optional)	4 tsp.	20 mL

Mix first 6 ingredients in shallow dish or on waxed paper.

Press dampened chicken into crumb mixture to coat completely.

Brown chicken in cooking oil in medium frying pan on medium-high for about 3 minutes per side. Reduce heat to medium-low.

Sprinkle Parmesan cheese over chicken. Cover. Cook for 10 to 20 minutes until chicken is no longer pink inside. Serves 4.

1 serving: 190 Calories; 6 g Total Fat; 470 mg Sodium; 28 g Protein; 4 g Carbohydrate; trace Dietary Fibre

Variation: Pour 2 cups (500 mL) spaghetti sauce into frying pan around browned chicken. Reduce heat to medium-low. Cover. Cook for about 30 minutes until chicken is no longer pink inside and sauce is bubbly. Sprinkle Parmesan cheese as above. Arrange 1 slice process mozzarella cheese over each chicken breast. Cover. Cook for 2 to 3 minutes until mozzarella cheese is melted.

Main Dishes

Chicken Tacos

Colourful variety. Messy to eat, but that's part of the fun. Not too spicy. Fresh tasting. Green chilies are mild. Avocado adds exotic flavour and look.

Boneless, skinless chicken thighs, cut into 1/4 inch (6 mm) strips	1 lb.	454 g
Cooking oil	1 tbsp.	15 mL
Can of diced green chilies, drained	4 oz.	113 g
Chili powder	1 tsp.	5 mL
Ground cumin	1/4 tsp.	1 mL
Salt	1/2 tsp.	2 mL
Taco shells	12	12
TOPPINGS		
Medium red onion, halved lengthwise and sliced	1/2	1/2
Medium tomato, seeded and cut into strips	1	1
Shredded lettuce	1 cup	250 mL
Sour cream (optional)	3/4 cup	175 mL
Ripe small avocado, peeled, pitted and cut into slivers (optional)	1	1

Sauté chicken in cooking oil in medium frying pan for 1 to 2 minutes until almost cooked.

Add green chilies, chili powder, cumin and salt. Stir-fry until no pink remains in chicken.

Divide chicken mixture among taco shells.

Toppings: Provide separate small bowls filled with toppings for each person to make their own. Makes 12 tacos.

1 taco: 127 Calories; 6.2 g Total Fat; 207 mg Sodium; 8 g Protein; 10 g Carbohydrate; 1 g Dietary Fibre

Pictured on page 36.

Crispy Fried Chicken

Definitely crispy with a pleasant and unexpected dill flavour. Chicken under the crispy crust is tender and so flavourful. Frying the chicken on the stove-top the old-fashioned way allows time to prepare a salad or side dish to go with it.

Hard margarine (or butter)	1/4 cup	60 mL
Cooking oil	1/4 cup	60 mL
Dill weed	2 tsp.	10 mL
Pepper	1/4 tsp.	1 mL
Garlic powder	1/4 tsp.	1 mL
Bone-in chicken parts, with skin	3 lbs.	1.4 kg

Heat first 5 ingredients in large frying pan on medium until margarine is melted. Stir.

Arrange chicken in single layer in margarine mixture. Cover. Cook for 15 minutes. Turn chicken over. Reduce heat to medium-low. Cover. Cook for 20 to 25 minutes, turning several times, until chicken is no longer pink. Remove to paper towels to drain. Serves 4 to 6.

1 serving: 693 Calories; 56.2 g Total Fat; 235 mg Sodium; 44 g Protein; trace Carbohydrate; trace Dietary Fibre

1. Orange Couscous And Green Beans, page 63
2. Sesame Broccoli, page 66
3. Hot Dilled Carrots, page 62

Props Courtesy Of: Pfaltzgraff Canada

Main Dishes

Wingin' It Wings

Hot finger food for any day of the week. Sweet glaze on top adds
sweetness to meat. Serve with Grilled Vegetable Salad, page 40,
or Creamed Niblets, page 65.

Whole chicken wings (about 24), tips removed and discarded	4 lbs.	1.8 kg
Apricot jam	1/2 cup	125 mL
Apple cider vinegar	1 1/2 tbsp.	25 mL
Onion powder	1/4 tsp.	1 mL
Garlic salt	1/4 tsp.	1 mL
Pepper	1/8 tsp.	0.5 mL
Paprika	1/4 tsp.	1 mL

Arrange chicken, skin-side down, in single layer on greased foil-lined
11 x 17 inch (28 x 43 cm) baking sheet. Bake in 425°F (220°C) oven for
20 minutes.

While wings are baking, mix remaining 6 ingredients in small bowl. Turn
wings over. Dab jam mixture on each wing. Bake for 10 minutes. Turn
wings. Dab remaining jam mixture over wings. Bake for 10 to 15 minutes
until tender. Serves 4.

1 serving: 696 Calories; 39.8 g Total Fat; 262 mg Sodium; 55 g Protein; 28 g Carbohydrate;
trace Dietary Fibre

1. Au Gratin Supper, page 120
2. Sole Salmon Rolls, page 100
3. Sautéed Spinach With Apricots,
   page 61

Chicken Cacciatore

Serve over buttered fettuccine with Salad Mix, page 43.
Start chicken searing first in pressure cooker, then chop the onion and peppers.

Bone-in, skinless chicken thighs (about 1 1/2 lbs., 680 g)	8	8
Olive (or cooking) oil	1 tbsp.	15 mL
Chopped onion	1 cup	250 mL
Chopped green pepper	1/2 cup	125 mL
Chopped red pepper	1/2 cup	125 mL
Garlic cloves, minced (or 1/2 tsp., 2 mL, powder)	2	2
Olive (or cooking) oil	1 tbsp.	15 mL
Can of diced tomatoes	28 oz.	796 mL
Red (or alcohol-free) wine	1/4 cup	60 mL
Tomato paste	2 tbsp.	30 mL
Granulated sugar	2 tsp.	10 mL
Water	1 tbsp.	15 mL
Cornstarch	1 tsp.	5 mL
Chopped fresh sweet basil leaves (or 1 tbsp., 15 mL, dried)	1/4 cup	60 mL
Pitted kalamata olives	1/4 cup	60 mL
Salt, sprinkle		
Pepper, sprinkle		

Sear chicken in first amount of olive oil in pressure cooker on medium-high for 3 minutes per side until golden. Remove from pressure cooker.

Sauté next 4 ingredients in second amount of olive oil in same pressure cooker for about 5 minutes until onion is soft.

Add chicken. Add next 4 ingredients. Stir. Lock lid in place. Bring pressure cooker up to pressure on medium-high. Reduce heat to medium just to maintain even pressure. Cook for 12 minutes. Allow pressure to drop naturally. Check to ensure chicken is no longer pink. Increase heat to medium-high.

Stir water into cornstarch in small cup until smooth. Stir into chicken mixture until boiling and slightly thickened.

Add basil, olives, salt and pepper. Stir. Serves 4.

1 serving: 327 Calories; 14.9 g Total Fat; 386 mg Sodium; 27 g Protein; 20 g Carbohydrate; 3 g Dietary Fibre

Pictured on page 107.

Turkey Schnitzel

Tender, moist pieces of turkey with a delicious, dark golden crumb coating.
Sauce is intense at first, but goes well with the schnitzel.

Large egg	1	1
Water	1 tbsp.	15 mL
Fine dry bread crumbs	1/2 cup	125 mL
Seasoned salt	1 1/2 tsp.	7 mL
Pepper	1/8 tsp.	0.5 mL
Cooking oil	1 tbsp.	15 mL
Hard margarine (or butter)	1 tbsp.	15 mL
Turkey breast cutlets (or scaloppini), about 1 lb. (454 g)	4	4
LEMON PEPPER SAUCE		
Dry white (or alcohol-free) wine	1/4 cup	60 mL
Lemon juice	2 tbsp.	30 mL
Parsley flakes	2 tsp.	10 mL
Lemon pepper	1/4 tsp.	1 mL

Beat egg and water with fork in small bowl.

Combine bread crumbs, seasoned salt and pepper in shallow dish or on waxed paper.

Heat cooking oil and margarine in medium frying pan on medium until margarine is melted.

While frying pan is heating, dip cutlets, 1 at a time, into egg mixture to coat. Press into crumb mixture to coat completely. Brown both sides of cutlets in hot oil mixture in frying pan for about 4 minutes per side until no longer pink. Transfer to serving plate. Keep warm.

Lemon Pepper Sauce: Stir wine, lemon juice, parsley and lemon pepper together in same frying pan. Bring to a boil. Reduce heat. Simmer, uncovered, for 2 minutes, scraping up any browned bits from pan, until sauce is reduced to about half. Drizzle over cutlets. Serves 4.

1 serving: 272 Calories; 9.2 g Total Fat; 675 mg Sodium; 31 g Protein; 12 g Carbohydrate; 1 g Dietary Fibre

Sweet And Sour Turkey

A thick dark sauce coating golden meatballs. A hint of rosemary in the meatballs. Using a small scoop works to speed up forming the meatballs. Perfect balance of sweet and sour. Serve with Orange Couscous And Green Beans, page 63, and a light salad.

Large egg, fork-beaten	1	1
Milk	1/4 cup	60 mL
Fine dry bread crumbs	1/2 cup	125 mL
Onion salt	1/2 tsp.	2 mL
Dried rosemary, crushed	1/2 tsp.	2 mL
Garlic powder	1/4 tsp.	1 mL
Ground turkey	1 lb.	454 g
SWEET AND SOUR SAUCE		
Brown sugar, packed	1/3 cup	75 mL
White vinegar	3 tbsp.	50 mL
Soy sauce	2 tbsp.	30 mL
Ketchup	2 tbsp.	30 mL
Garlic powder	1/4 tsp.	1 mL
Ground ginger	1/4 tsp.	1 mL

Stir first 6 ingredients together in medium bowl.

Add ground turkey. Mix well. Shape into 1 inch (2.5 cm) balls. Arrange on greased baking sheet. Bake in 375°F (190°C) oven for 15 minutes.

Sweet And Sour Sauce: While meatballs are cooking, heat and stir all 6 ingredients in large frying pan on medium for 3 to 4 minutes until boiling. Add baked meatballs. Simmer, uncovered, for about 5 minutes until sauce is thickened and meatballs are coated. Makes about 40 meatballs. Serves 6.

1 serving: 218 Calories; 7.4 g Total Fat; 654 mg Sodium; 16 g Protein; 22 g Carbohydrate; trace Dietary Fibre

Tarragon-Topped Fish

Creamy topping mimics a hollandaise sauce and broils to a nice light brown. Tarragon adds a sweetness that offsets any saltiness. Serve with Pickled Beet Salad, page 42.

Fresh (or frozen, thawed) white fish fillets (such as cod or sole), cut into 4 equal pieces	1 lb.	454 g
Paprika	1/2 tsp.	2 mL
Pepper, sprinkle		
Mayonnaise (not salad dressing)	1/4 cup	60 mL
Lemon juice	2 tsp.	10 mL
Dried tarragon	1/8 tsp.	0.5 mL

Place sheet of foil over broiler tray or in baking pan large enough to hold fish in single layer. Spray foil with cooking spray. Arrange fish in single layer on foil. Sprinkle paprika and pepper over fish. Broil 5 to 6 inches (12.5 to 15 cm) from heat for 4 minutes.

Meanwhile, mix mayonnaise, lemon juice and tarragon in small bowl. Divide and spread over fish. Broil for 6 to 8 minutes until fish flakes easily when tested with fork and topping is lightly browned. Serves 4.

1 serving: 202 Calories; 12.6 g Total Fat; 137 mg Sodium; 20 g Protein; 1 g Carbohydrate; trace Dietary Fibre

Paré Pointer
So many sneezes are often pointed at-choo.

Red Tuna Sauce

*Pretty when served over linguine and garnished with
chopped fresh parsley and ripe pitted olives.
Sauce adheres well. Cook pasta while making sauce.*

Finely chopped onion	1/2 cup	125 mL
Olive (or cooking) oil	1 tbsp.	15 mL
Garlic cloves, minced (or 1/2 tsp., 2 mL, powder)	2	2
All-purpose flour	1 tbsp.	15 mL
Skim evaporated milk	1 cup	250 mL
Jar of red peppers, drained	14 oz.	398 mL
Granulated sugar	1/2 tsp.	2 mL
Dried sweet basil	1/2 tsp.	2 mL
Salt	1/2 tsp.	2 mL
Cayenne pepper (optional)	1/16 tsp.	0.5 mL
Cans of solid white tuna, packed in water (6 1/2 oz., 184 g, each), drained and broken into chunks	2	2

Sauté onion in olive oil in large non-stick frying pan for about 3 minutes until soft.

Add garlic. Sauté for 1 minute. Sprinkle with flour. Stir well.

Gradually add evaporated milk, stirring constantly. Heat and stir for about 5 minutes until boiling and thickened.

Put red peppers into blender. Process until smooth. Add to milk mixture.

Add sugar, basil, salt and cayenne pepper. Reduce heat to medium-low. Stir in tuna. Cook for about 5 minutes, stirring occasionally, until heated through. Makes 4 cups (1 L) sauce. Serves 4.

1 serving: 209 Calories; 6.1 g Total Fat; 1273 mg Sodium; 24 g Protein; 14 g Carbohydrate; trace Dietary Fibre

Pictured on front cover.

Variation: Omit dried sweet basil. Add 2 tsp. (10 mL) basil pesto.

(30 minutes) Fish And Shrimp Bake

Chunks of fish and shrimp in a light-textured, green-flecked sauce.
Flavour of fish comes through delicately with just a hint of mustard.
Serve with rice or pasta and a salad.

Frozen white fish fillets (such as cod or sole)	1 lb.	454 g
Raw medium shrimp (about 3 oz., 85 g), peeled and deveined	12	12
WINE MUSTARD SAUCE		
Hard margarine (or butter), melted	2 tbsp.	30 mL
Grainy mustard	1 tbsp.	15 mL
Green onion, sliced	1	1
Chopped fresh parsley	2 tbsp.	30 mL
White (or alcohol-free) wine	1/2 cup	125 mL
Lemon pepper	1/4 tsp.	1 mL
Salt	1/4 tsp.	1 mL

Cut fish into 12 pieces. Place in ungreased 1 quart (1 L) shallow casserole. Add shrimp.

Wine Mustard Sauce: Combine all 7 ingredients in small bowl. Pour over fish mixture. Stir. Bake, uncovered, in 425°F (220°C) oven for 15 minutes until fish flakes easily when tested with fork. Serves 4.

1 serving: 225 Calories; 9 g Total Fat; 364 mg Sodium; 28 g Protein; 1 g Carbohydrate; trace Dietary Fibre

Variation: After cooking, remove fish and shrimp to serving dish using slotted spoon. Keep warm. Transfer liquid in casserole to medium saucepan. Boil on medium-high for 5 to 10 minutes until reduced and slightly thickened. Drizzle sauce over fish and shrimp.

Pictured on page 108.

Paré Pointer

After seeing a submarine, the sardine said, "There goes a can of people."

Dressed-Up Fish Sticks

Three ways to dress up a favourite rush-hour food.

DILLED FISH STICKS

Creamy cucumber salad dressing	3/4 cup	175 mL
Dill weed	1 tsp.	5 mL
Frozen fish sticks	12	12

Combine salad dressing and dill weed in shallow dish. Add fish sticks. Stir to coat. Arrange in single layer on greased baking sheet. Bake in 425°F (220°C) oven for 5 minutes. Turn over. Bake for 5 minutes. Makes 12 fish sticks.

1 fish stick: 149 Calories; 11.2 g Total Fat; 318 mg Sodium; 5 g Protein; 7 g Carbohydrate; 0 g Dietary Fibre

CAESAR FISH STICKS

Caesar salad dressing	3/4 cup	175 mL
Grated Parmesan cheese	1 tbsp.	15 mL
Frozen fish sticks	12	12

Combine salad dressing and Parmesan cheese in shallow dish. Add fish sticks. Stir to coat. Arrange in single layer on greased baking sheet. Bake in 425°F (220°C) oven for 5 minutes. Turn over. Bake for 5 minutes. Makes 12 fish sticks.

1 fish stick: 151 Calories; 11.4 g Total Fat; 328 mg Sodium; 5 g Protein; 7 g Carbohydrate; 0 g Dietary Fibre

PIZZA FISH STICKS

Pizza sauce	3/4 cup	175 mL
Grated Parmesan cheese	1 tbsp.	15 mL
Frozen fish sticks	12	12
Mozzarella cheese, sliced to fit	3/4 lb.	340 g

Combine pizza sauce and Parmesan cheese in shallow dish. Add fish sticks. Stir to coat. Arrange in single layer on greased baking sheet. Bake in 425°F (220°C) oven for 5 minutes. Turn over. Bake for 5 minutes.

Lay mozzarella cheese on fish sticks. Let stand for 2 minutes until cheese is melted. Makes 12 fish sticks.

1 fish stick: 179 Calories; 10.7 g Total Fat; 363 mg Sodium; 11 g Protein; 10 g Carbohydrate; trace Dietary Fibre

Cod In Dill Sauce

Good dill flavour with the delicate taste of onion. Fish is tender and juicy.
Thicker fillets will need additional time to bake.

DILL SAUCE

Hard margarine (or butter)	1 tbsp.	15 mL
All-purpose flour	1 tbsp.	15 mL
Milk	1/4 cup	60 mL
Dill weed	3/4 tsp.	4 mL
Onion powder	1/4 tsp.	1 mL
Dried rosemary, crushed	1/4 tsp.	1 mL
Salt	1/4 tsp.	1 mL
Pepper	1/8 tsp.	0.5 mL
Frozen cod fillets (1 lb., 454 g)	4	4

Dill Sauce: Melt margarine in small saucepan. Mix in flour until smooth. Add next 6 ingredients. Heat and stir until boiling and very thick.

Arrange fillets in single layer in greased shallow pan. Spread sauce over fillets. Cook in 425°F (220°C) oven for 15 to 20 minutes until fish flakes easily when tested with fork. Serves 4.

1 serving: 134 Calories; 3.9 g Total Fat; 252 mg Sodium; 21 g Protein; 3 g Carbohydrate; trace Dietary Fibre

 tip   *Prepare and bake all-in-one meals like casseroles in advance when you have some extra time. Freeze and reheat on those extra busy days.*

Sole Salmon Rolls

Unique way of serving fish. Great for any day of the week.
Serve with Sautéed Spinach With Apricots, page 61.

Sole fillets (about 2 lbs., 900 g)	8	8
Block of cream cheese, softened	4 oz.	125 g
Lemon juice	1 tsp.	5 mL
Prepared horseradish	1 tsp.	5 mL
Onion salt	1/2 tsp.	2 mL
Liquid smoke (optional)	1/2 tsp.	2 mL
Can of red salmon, drained, skin and round bones removed	7 1/2 oz.	213 g
Water	3/4 cup	175 mL
White (or alcohol-free) wine (or apple juice)	1/4 cup	60 mL
Onion salt	1/2 tsp.	2 mL
Hard margarine (or butter)	2 tbsp.	30 mL
All-purpose flour	3 tbsp.	50 mL
Salt, sprinkle		
Pepper, sprinkle		
Fresh chopped parsley, for garnish		

Lay fillets on work surface. Blot dry using paper towels.

Mash cream cheese, lemon juice, horseradish, first amount of onion salt and liquid smoke together in medium bowl until well mixed and smooth.

Add salmon. Mix well. Divide and spread over fillets. Roll up each fillet. Secure with wooden picks.

Combine water, wine and second amount of onion salt in medium saucepan. Stand fish rolls in wine mixture. Bring liquid to a boil. Reduce heat to medium. Cover. Gently simmer for 5 minutes until fish is white and opaque. Gently remove rolls from liquid to serving platter using slotted spoon. Keep warm. Strain liquid. Reserve for sauce.

(continued on next page)

Melt margarine in same saucepan. Stir in flour until smooth. Heat and stir for 1 minute. Add reserved liquid. Heat and stir until boiling and thickened.

Sprinkle salt and pepper over sauce. Stir. Makes about 1 cup (250 mL) sauce. Pour over fish rolls.

Garnish with parsley. Serves 8.

1 serving: 241 Calories; 12.2 g Total Fat; 424 mg Sodium; 27 g Protein; 3 g Carbohydrate; trace Dietary Fibre

Pictured on page 90.

Baked Fish Fillets

A spicy bite from the cayenne pepper; a tangy taste from the lemon juice.

Finely chopped onion	1/4 cup	60 mL
Hard margarine (or butter)	1 tbsp.	15 mL
Fish fillets	1 lb.	454 g
Lemon juice	3 tbsp.	50 mL
Cayenne pepper	1/8 tsp.	0.5 mL
Salt	1/4 tsp.	1 mL

Sauté onion in margarine in medium frying pan for about 3 minutes until golden.

While onion is sautéing, arrange fillets in single layer in greased 9 x 13 inch (22 x 33 cm) pan.

Add lemon juice, cayenne pepper and salt to onion. Stir. Spoon over fillets, being sure to get some on every piece. Bake, uncovered, on centre rack in 450°F (230°C) oven for about 10 minutes until fish flakes easily when tested with fork. Serves 4.

1 serving: 126 Calories; 3.7 g Total Fat; 244 mg Sodium; 20 g Protein; 2 g Carbohydrate; trace Dietary Fibre

Salmon And Sun-Dried Tomato Pasta

You will be surprised and pleased how delicious and moist salmon is when microwaved. This creamy pasta makes a great dish for any time of year.

Medium bow pasta (about 12 oz., 340 g, uncooked)	5 cups	1.25 L
Boiling water	12 cups	3 L
Cooking oil	1 tbsp.	15 mL
Small red onion, chopped	1	1
Garlic cloves, minced (or 1/2 tsp., 2 mL, powder)	2	2
Whipping cream	1 cup	250 mL
Prepared chicken broth	1/3 cup	75 mL
Salmon fillet, skin removed, halved	1 lb.	454 g
Fresh spinach leaves, stems removed, lightly packed	2 cups	500 mL
Sun-dried tomatoes in oil, drained and sliced	2/3 cup	150 mL
Finely grated Parmesan cheese	1/2 cup	125 mL
Chopped fresh parsley (or 1 tbsp., 15 mL, flakes)	1/4 cup	60 mL
Salt, sprinkle		
Pepper, sprinkle		

Cook pasta in boiling water in large uncovered pot or Dutch oven for 8 to 10 minutes until tender but firm. Drain. Turn pasta into large bowl.

While pasta is cooking, combine cooking oil, red onion and garlic in large microwave-safe dish. Cover. Microwave on high (100%) for about 3 minutes, stirring once during cooking, until onion is soft.

Add whipping cream and broth. Mix.

Lay salmon over onion mixture. Cover. Microwave on high (100%) for 3 minutes.

(continued on next page)

Layer spinach and tomato over salmon. Cover. Microwave on high (100%) for about 3 minutes until spinach is wilted and salmon flakes easily when tested with fork. Flake salmon in dish, removing any bones and skin. Stir salmon, spinach and tomato. Add to pasta in bowl.

Add Parmesan cheese and parsley. Mix well.

Sprinkle salt and pepper over pasta mixture. Makes 8 cups (2 L).

1 cup (250 mL): 533 Calories; 22.6 g Total Fat; 246 mg Sodium; 25 g Protein; 57 g Carbohydrate; 3 g Dietary Fibre

Pictured on page 125.

Quick Fish

Onion is the predominant flavour in this very fast-to-prepare dish.

Frozen fish fillets	1 lb.	454 g
Envelope of dry onion soup mix (1 1/4 oz., 38 g, size), stir before measuring	1/2	1/2
Ketchup	1 tbsp.	15 mL
Cooking oil	1 tbsp.	15 mL

Arrange fillets in microwave-safe dish large enough to hold in single layer (a large plate works well).

Combine soup mix, ketchup and cooking oil in small bowl. Spoon over fillets, being sure to get some on every piece. Cover. Microwave on high (100%) for about 10 minutes, turning dish and fillets at halftime if microwave doesn't have turntable, until fish flakes easily when tested with fork. Rearrange fillets at halftime so outside edges are inside and inside edges are outside. Serves 4.

1 serving: 142 Calories; 4.5 g Total Fat; 532 mg Sodium; 21 g Protein; 4 g Carbohydrate; trace Dietary Fibre

Shrimp And Mushroom Stir-Fry

A great taste combination that's quick to prepare. Very flavourful. Crunchy.

Cornstarch	1 tbsp.	15 mL
Soy sauce	2 tbsp.	30 mL
Granulated sugar	2 tsp.	10 mL
Water	2 tbsp.	30 mL
Chicken bouillon powder	1/4 tsp.	1 mL
Cooking oil	2 tbsp.	30 mL
Slices of gingerroot	2	2
Garlic clove, halved	1	1
Sliced fresh mushrooms (about 5 cups, 1.25 L)	1 lb.	454 g
Fresh bean sprouts (about 4 cups, 1 L)	12 oz.	340 g
Sliced green onion	1/2 cup	125 mL
Cooked salad (or cocktail) shrimp (about 12 oz., 340 g), fresh or frozen, thawed	1 1/2 cups	375 mL

Combine first 5 ingredients in small bowl. Set aside.

Heat cooking oil in wok or large frying pan on medium. Add ginger and garlic. Stir-fry for 1 to 2 minutes until golden. Remove and discard ginger and garlic with slotted spoon. Increase heat to medium-high.

Add mushrooms. Stir-fry for 3 minutes until soft.

Add bean sprouts and green onion. Stir-fry for 4 minutes.

Add shrimp. Heat and stir until heated through. Stir reserved cornstarch mixture. Push vegetable mixture to side of wok to expose liquid. Stir cornstarch mixture into liquid until boiling and thickened. Stir in vegetables until coated. Makes 5 cups (1.25 L). Serves 4.

1 serving: 171 Calories; 7.9 g Total Fat; 639 mg Sodium; 12 g Protein; 16 g Carbohydrate; 3 g Dietary Fibre

Variation: Add 1/2 medium red pepper, slivered, with bean sprouts.

Double Fish Fry

Fry the topping and then fry the fish. Very flavourful. A little sweet with a subtle rosemary flavour. Crumb topping adds nice colour and flavour.

Small onion, thinly sliced and separated into rings	1	1
Cooking oil	2 tbsp.	30 mL
Fine dry bread crumbs	1/2 cup	125 mL
Dried rosemary, crushed	1 tsp.	5 mL
Haddock (or halibut) fillets (1 lb., 454 g)	4	4
Cooking oil	1 tbsp.	15 mL
Salt, sprinkle		
Pepper, sprinkle		
Half-and-half cream	3/4 cup	175 mL

Sauté onion in first amount of cooking oil in medium frying pan until golden.

Add bread crumbs and rosemary. Heat and stir for 2 minutes. Transfer to plate.

Brown fillets on 1 side in second amount of cooking oil in same frying pan.

Sprinkle with salt and pepper. Scatter onion mixture over fillets.

Pour cream around edge of frying pan. Cover. Simmer for about 3 minutes until fish flakes easily when tested with fork. Serves 4.

1 serving: 311 Calories; 16.8 g Total Fat; 221 mg Sodium; 25 g Protein; 14 g Carbohydrate; 1 g Dietary Fibre

Paré Pointer
If you swallow a spoon, sit still and don't stir.

Dilled Fish

Poached fish can be prepared even if you forgot to thaw it! Mild flavours.
Fish is tender and moist. Serve with Sweet Potato With Basil, page 64.

Package of frozen cod fillets	14 oz.	400 g
Hot water, to cover		
DILL SAUCE		
Sour cream	1/2 cup	125 mL
Salad dressing (or mayonnaise)	1/2 cup	125 mL
White vinegar	1/4 tsp.	1 mL
Dried chives	1 1/2 tbsp.	25 mL
Dill weed	1 tsp.	5 mL
Cayenne pepper	1/8 tsp.	0.5 mL

Set fillets in large pot or Dutch oven. Cover with hot water. Bring to a boil on high. Reduce heat to medium. Cover. Simmer for about 4 minutes until fish flakes easily when tested with fork. Drain. Transfer to large plate or divide among 4 dinner plates.

Dill Sauce: While fish is cooking, stir all 6 ingredients together in small bowl. Makes 1 cup (250 mL) sauce. Serve warm or chilled over fish. Serves 4.

1 serving: 305 Calories; 20.4 g Total Fat; 266 mg Sodium; 20 g Protein; 10 g Carbohydrate; trace Dietary Fibre

1. Beef And Sprouts, page 68
2. Saucy Oriental Dinner, page 118
3. Chicken Cacciatore, page 92

Stove-Top Bean Casserole

A quick and easy meatless dish. A bit of sauce coats every item.
Wonderfully healthy. Curry flavour prominent with a bit of sweetness
from the sugar and pear. Great on its own, with a baked potato or with rice.

Can of mixed beans, drained and rinsed	19 oz.	540 mL
Can of stewed tomatoes	14 oz.	398 mL
Ripe pear, peeled and diced	1	1
Chopped onion	1 cup	250 mL
Water	1/3 cup	75 mL
Granulated sugar	1 tbsp.	15 mL
Curry powder	1 tsp.	5 mL
Dried whole oregano	1/4 tsp.	1 mL
Dried sweet basil	1/4 tsp.	1 mL

Combine all 9 ingredients in large saucepan. Bring to a boil. Reduce heat to medium. Simmer, uncovered, for about 20 minutes until pear and onion are tender and sauce has thickened. Makes 3 1/2 cups (875 mL).

3/4 cup (175 mL): 131 Calories, 0.8 g Total Fat; 363 mg Sodium; 6 g Protein; 27 g Carbohydrate; 5 g Dietary Fibre

1. Skillet Supper, page 75
2. Popeye Pasta, page 112
3. Fish And Shrimp Bake, page 97

Perogies With Mushroom Sauce

Enough rich, flavourful sauce to generously coat perogies.
Serve as a main course or as a side dish. Serve with salad and kielbasa.

Package of sliced fresh mushrooms	8 oz.	227 g
Green onions, sliced	3	3
Garlic cloves, minced (or 1/2 tsp., 2 mL, powder)	2	2
Hard margarine (or butter)	1/4 cup	60 mL
Bag of frozen potato and Cheddar cheese perogies	2.2 lbs.	1 kg
Boiling water	16 cups	4 L
Salt	1 tbsp.	15 mL
All-purpose flour	2 tbsp.	30 mL
White (or alcohol-free) wine	1/3 cup	75 mL
Water	2/3 cup	150 mL
Vegetable (or chicken) bouillon powder	1 tbsp.	15 mL
Dill weed	1/2 tsp.	2 mL
Dried marjoram	1/4 tsp.	1 mL
Half-and-half cream (or evaporated milk)	2/3 cup	150 mL
Finely grated Asiago cheese (optional)	1/4 cup	60 mL

Sauté mushrooms, green onion and garlic in margarine in large frying pan for about 6 minutes until liquid from mushrooms has evaporated and mushrooms are turning brown. Reduce heat to medium.

Meanwhile, drop perogies into boiling water and salt in large pot or Dutch oven. Gently stir to keep from sticking to bottom. Bring to a boil. Boil, uncovered, for about 4 minutes until perogies bob to surface. Drain. Return to pot.

While perogies are cooking, sprinkle flour over mushroom mixture. Stir well. Slowly stir in wine until boiling and thickened.

Add water, bouillon powder, dill weed and marjoram. Heat and stir until mixture is boiling and thickened.

(continued on next page)

Main Dishes

Stir in cream. Bring to a simmer. Add to perogies. Toss to coat. Turn into serving bowl.

Sprinkle Asiago cheese over perogy mixture. Serves 5 to 6.

1 serving: 532 Calories; 28.5 g Total Fat; 1250 mg Sodium; 16 g Protein; 51 g Carbohydrate; 2 g Dietary Fibre

Meatless Chili

Colourful, thick and hearty. Nice balance of flavours with just a little heat. Increase chili powder if more heat is desired.

Medium onion, chopped	1	1
Garlic clove, minced (or 1/4 tsp., 1 mL, powder)	1	1
Cooking oil	1 tbsp.	15 mL
Cans of kidney beans (14 oz., 398 mL, each), drained	2	2
Can of diced tomatoes, with juice	14 oz.	398 mL
Ketchup	1/4 cup	60 mL
Medium green or red pepper, chopped	1	1
Can of sliced mushrooms, drained (or 2 cups, 500 mL, fresh, sliced)	10 oz.	284 ml
Small eggplant, peeled and diced	1	1
Brown sugar, packed	2 tbsp.	30 mL
Chili powder	1 1/2 tbsp.	25 mL
Salt	1 tsp.	5 mL
Pepper	1/4 tsp.	1 mL
Ground cumin	1/4 tsp.	1 mL
Chopped fresh cilantro (or parsley), for garnish		

Sauté onion and garlic in cooking oil in large pot or Dutch oven until onion is soft and golden.

Add next 11 ingredients. Stir. Bring to a boil on medium-high, stirring frequently. Reduce heat to medium. Simmer, uncovered, for about 10 minutes, stirring occasionally, until heated through.

Garnish with cilantro. Makes 6 cups (1.5 L).

1 cup (250 mL): 201 Calories; 3.5 g Total Fat; 933 mg Sodium; 9 g Protein; 37 g Carbohydrate; 7 g Dietary Fibre

Pictured on page 72.

Popeye Pasta

Casual in looks, good in flavour. Fresh-tasting garlic and tomato with salty feta cheese. A Mediterranean look and taste.

Angel hair (or capellini) pasta	8 oz.	225 g
Boiling water	12 cups	3 L
Salt	1 tbsp.	15 mL
Olive (or cooking) oil	1 tbsp.	15 mL
Diced roma (plum) tomato	2 cups	500 mL
Garlic cloves, minced (or 3/4 tsp., 4 mL, powder)	3	3
Olive (or cooking) oil	2 tbsp.	30 mL
Coarsely chopped fresh spinach, lightly packed	3 cups	750 mL
Balsamic vinegar	1 tbsp.	15 mL
Chopped fresh marjoram (or 3/4 tsp., 4 mL, dried)	1 tbsp.	15 mL
Salt	1/2 tsp.	2 mL
Granulated sugar, just a pinch		
Pepper, sprinkle		
Crumbled feta cheese	1 cup	250 mL

Cook pasta in boiling water and first amount of salt in large uncovered pot or Dutch oven for 6 minutes until tender but firm. Drain. Return to pot.

Add first amount of olive oil. Toss. Keep warm.

Meanwhile, sauté tomato and garlic in second amount of olive oil in large frying pan for about 2 minutes until tomatoes have released their juices.

Add next 6 ingredients. Heat and stir for about 1 minute just until spinach is wilted and heated through.

Pour over pasta. Add feta cheese. Toss well. Makes 5 cups (1.25 L). Serves 4.

1 serving: 406 Calories; 16.9 g Total Fat; 800 mg Sodium; 15 g Protein; 50 g Carbohydrate; 3 g Dietary Fibre

Pictured on page 108.

Lamburgers

Here's a chance to add another burger to your repertoire.

Fine dry bread crumbs	1/3 cup	75 mL
Dried whole oregano	1/2 tsp.	2 mL
Seasoned salt	1/2 tsp.	2 mL
Pepper	1/4 tsp.	1 mL
Crumbled feta cheese (about 3 oz., 85 g)	1/2 cup	125 mL
Milk	1/4 cup	60 mL
Lean ground lamb	1 lb.	454 g
Hamburger buns, split (buttered, optional)	4	4

Mix first 6 ingredients in medium bowl.

Add ground lamb. Mix well. Divide and shape into 4 patties. Cook in non-stick frying pan on medium-low for about 15 minutes per side until no pink remains in centre.

Place patties in buns. Serves 4.

1 serving: 448 Calories; 23 g Total Fat; 788 mg Sodium; 28 g Protein; 30 g Carbohydrate; trace Dietary Fibre

 Marinades are used to flavour and tenderize more economical, and often tougher, cuts of meat. Most marinades contain an acid ingredient (lemon juice, tomato juice, vinegar or wine) which helps to break down the sinewy muscle in these cuts of meat. For this reason, the marinade should completely cover the meat. If there is not enough marinade to do so, then turn the food every so often.

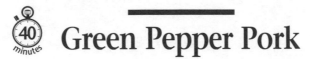

Green Pepper Pork

Prepared in the pressure cooker. Has great pepper taste.
Serve over buttered noodles or with steamed rice.

Sliced brown (cremini) mushrooms	4 cups	1 L
Cooking oil	1 tbsp.	15 mL
Cooking oil	1 tbsp.	15 mL
Pork tenderloin, cut into 1 inch (2.5 cm) cubes	1 1/2 lbs.	680 g
Chicken broth	1/2 cup	125 mL
Grainy mustard	2 tbsp.	30 mL
Chopped fresh thyme leaves (not dried)	2 tbsp.	30 mL
Whole green peppercorns in brine, drained and lightly crushed	1 tbsp.	15 mL
Finely grated orange zest	1 tsp.	5 mL
Ground nutmeg	1/4 tsp.	1 mL
Sour cream	1/3 cup	75 mL

Sauté mushrooms in first amount of cooking oil in pressure cooker on medium for about 5 minutes until browned. Remove from pressure cooker. Set aside.

Heat second amount of cooking oil in pressure cooker on medium-high. Sear pork, in 2 batches, for about 5 minutes until browned.

Add next 6 ingredients. Stir. Lock lid in place. Bring pressure cooker up to pressure on medium-high. Reduce heat to medium-low just to maintain even pressure. Cook for 12 minutes. Remove from heat. Allow pressure to drop naturally. Remove lid. Check to ensure pork is tender.

Add mushrooms and sour cream. Stir. Serves 4.

1 serving: 376 Calories; 21.6 g Total Fat; 305 mg Sodium; 39 g Protein; 6 g Carbohydrate; 1 g Dietary Fibre

Main Dishes

Handy Dandy Dish

This appetizing main dish uses convenience foods from your pantry.
Make a salad while this is cooking.

Box of scalloped potato mix	5 1/2 oz.	149 g
Water	2 cups	500 mL
Milk	3/4 cup	175 mL
Frozen peas	2 cups	500 mL
Frozen brown-and-serve sausages, cut into 1/2 inch (12 mm) pieces	8 oz.	225 g

Empty scalloped potato mix into large frying pan. Add water and milk. Stir. Bring to a gentle boil. Reduce heat. Cover. Simmer for about 30 minutes, stirring occasionally, until potatoes are tender.

Add peas and sausage. Stir. Cover. Simmer for about 10 minutes until peas are tender and sausage is heated through. Serves 4.

1 serving: 401 Calories; 19.6 g Total Fat; 1093 mg Sodium; 14 g Protein; 43 g Carbohydrate; 5 g Dietary Fibre

Mix up a large batch of your favourite hamburger patties. Shape into patties and place on waxed paper-lined baking sheets in single layer. Place, uncovered, in freezer overnight. In the morning, remove frozen patties to large resealable freezer bag. Label and place in freezer. Take out as many individual patties as you need for a quick barbecue meal.

Sweet And Sour Sausage Supper

Good combination of flavours. More sweet than sour.
Easy and economical. Very tasty.

Long grain white rice	1 cup	250 mL
Water	2 cups	500 mL
Salt	1 tsp.	5 mL
Breakfast sausages, cut into 1/2 inch (12 mm) coins	1 lb.	454 g
Chopped onion	1 cup	250 mL
Chopped celery	1/2 cup	125 mL
Small green pepper, chopped	1	1
Jar of sweet and sour sauce (your favourite)	12 oz.	341 mL
Soy sauce (optional)	1 tbsp.	15 mL

Cook rice in water and salt in medium saucepan for 15 to 20 minutes until tender and liquid is absorbed. Keep warm.

Meanwhile, cook sausage in medium frying pan until lightly browned. Remove with slotted spoon to paper towels to drain, reserving 1 tbsp. (15 mL) drippings in frying pan. Discard remaining drippings.

Add onion, celery and green pepper to reserved drippings. Sauté until tender-crisp.

Add sausage and both sauces. Heat, stirring once or twice, until boiling. Arrange rice on serving platter. Pour sausage mixture in centre. Serves 4.

1 serving: 523 Calories; 19.8 g Total Fat; 1322 mg Sodium; 12 g Protein; 73 g Carbohydrate; 2 g Dietary Fibre

---

Paré Pointer
If a flea lands on a rabbit, you have a bugs bunny.

Moment's Notice Stir-Fry

With canned and frozen staples on hand, you can whip up a meal in no time.
Sweet mustard-tasting sauce. Colourful. Chunky. Very tasty.

SAUCE		
Prepared orange juice	1/2 cup	125 mL
Cornstarch	1 tbsp.	15 mL
Brown sugar, packed	1/4 cup	60 mL
Prepared mustard	2 tsp.	10 mL
Cooking oil	1 tsp.	5 mL
Can of processed meat, cut into 3/4 inch (2 cm) cubes	12 oz.	340 g
Can of potatoes, drained and cut into chunks	19 oz.	540 mL
Frozen mixed vegetables (your favourite)	4 cups	1 L
Can of baby corn, drained	14 oz.	398 mL
Can of french-fried onions	2 3/4 oz.	79 g

Sauce: Stir orange juice into cornstarch in small bowl until smooth. Stir in brown sugar and mustard. Set aside.

Heat cooking oil in wok or large frying pan on medium-high until hot. Add meat. Stir-fry for about 2 minutes until lightly browned. Transfer to bowl, using slotted spoon, leaving drippings in frying pan.

Add potato, mixed vegetables and corn to drippings. Stir. Cover. Cook on medium-high for about 8 minutes, stirring twice, until vegetables are tender. Stir orange juice mixture. Add to potato mixture. Heat and stir until boiling and thickened. Add meat. Stir until heated through. Turn out onto serving platter.

Sprinkle french-fried onions over vegetable mixture just before serving. Makes 8 cups (2 L). Serves 4.

1 serving: 502 Calories; 12.9 g Total Fat; 1539 mg Sodium; 25 g Protein; 79 g Carbohydrate; 8 g Dietary Fibre

⏱ (30) Saucy Oriental Dinner

Nicely coloured. Thick rich sauce. Pork is tender and full of flavour.
Vegetables are tender-crisp. Sauce is pleasantly balanced with a hint of garlic.

Rice vermicelli, broken up	6 oz.	170 g
Boiling water		
ORIENTAL SAUCE		
Water	1 cup	250 mL
Soy sauce	3 tbsp.	50 mL
Liquid honey	2 tbsp.	30 mL
Hoisin sauce	1 tbsp.	15 mL
Sambal oelek (chili paste)	1/2 tsp.	2 mL
Garlic cloves, minced (or 1/2 tsp., 2 mL, powder)	2	2
Cornstarch	4 tsp.	20 mL
Cooking oil	1 tbsp.	15 mL
Pork tenderloin, cut into 1/2 inch (12 mm) cubes	1 lb.	454 g
Bag of chopped fresh oriental mixed vegetables (about 4 cups, 1 L), see Note	1 lb.	454 g
Sliced green onion (optional)	1/4 cup	60 mL

Cover vermicelli with boiling water in medium bowl. Let stand for 2 minutes until softened. Drain.

Oriental Sauce: While vermicelli is soaking, combine first 7 ingredients in small dish. Set aside. Makes 1 1/4 cups (300 mL) sauce.

Heat cooking oil in wok or large frying pan on medium-high until hot. Add pork. Stir-fry for 3 minutes.

Add vegetables. Stir-fry for 3 to 4 minutes until vegetables are tender-crisp. Stir sauce. Add to pork mixture. Heat and stir for about 4 minutes until boiling and slightly thickened. Add vermicelli. Toss. Heat for 2 to 3 minutes until heated through.

(continued on next page)

118 Main Dishes

Sprinkle green onion over pork mixture. Makes 6 cups (1.5 L). Serves 4.

1 serving: 455 Calories; 11.3 g Total Fat; 1047 mg Sodium; 30 g Protein; 59 g Carbohydrate; 2 g Dietary Fibre

Pictured on page 107.

Note: Oriental mixed vegetables include any mix of peppers, broccoli, cauliflower, pea pods, bok choy, cabbage, bean sprouts or other vegetables.

Creamed Pork Chops

A honey mustard cream sauce accompanies these pan-fried pork chops. Tender and juicy. Serve with Quickest Mashed Potatoes, page 66.

Sour cream	1/2 cup	125 mL
All-purpose flour	2 tsp.	10 mL
Prepared mustard	1 tbsp.	15 mL
Liquid honey	2 tbsp.	30 mL
Bone-in pork loin chops (about 1 1/2 lbs., 680 g), 1/2 inch (12 mm) thick, trimmed of fat	4	4
Cooking oil	1 tbsp.	15 mL
Salt, sprinkle		
Pepper, sprinkle		
Water	3/4 cup	175 mL
Beef bouillon powder	2 tsp.	10 mL

Stir sour cream into flour in small cup until smooth. Add mustard and honey. Stir. Set aside.

Brown pork chops in cooking oil in large frying pan on medium-high for 2 to 3 minutes per side until tender. Sprinkle salt and pepper over pork chops. Remove to serving platter. Keep warm.

Add water to same frying pan. Add bouillon powder. Heat and stir, scraping up any browned bits from pan, until boiling. Slowly stir sour cream mixture into water mixture until slightly thickened. Pour sauce over pork chops or serve on the side. Serves 4.

1 serving: 276 Calories; 13.7 g Total Fat; 436 mg Sodium; 26 g Protein; 12 g Carbohydrate; trace Dietary Fibre

Au Gratin Supper

Uses all pantry and freezer items. Good ham flavour. Lots of fresh-tasting peas.

Box of au gratin scalloped potato mix	5 oz.	141 g
Can of flaked ham, with liquid, broken up	6 1/2 oz.	184 g
Frozen peas	2 cups	500 mL

Prepare potatoes according to package directions in large saucepan, cooking for only about 10 minutes until potatoes are not quite done and still firm.

Add ham and peas. Stir. Bring to a boil. Reduce heat. Cover. Simmer for 4 to 5 minutes until potatoes and peas are fully cooked. Makes 4 1/4 cups (1 L). Serves 4.

1 serving: 246 Calories; 5.3 g Total Fat; 1124 mg Sodium; 14 g Protein; 37 g Carbohydrate; 5 g Dietary Fibre

Pictured on page 90.

Pork Chops With Apple

Apples are sweet and tender.

Bone-in pork loin chops (about 1 1/2 lbs., 680 g), 1/2 inch (12 mm) thick, trimmed of fat	4	4
Cooking oil	1 tbsp.	15 mL
Salt, sprinkle		
Pepper, sprinkle		
Medium cooking apples (such as McIntosh), peeled and sliced	2	2
Granulated sugar	1/4 cup	60 mL

Brown pork chops in cooking oil in large frying pan on medium-high for 2 to 3 minutes per side until tender. Sprinkle with salt and pepper. Remove to serving platter. Keep warm.

(continued on next page)

120   Main Dishes

Add apple and sugar to same frying pan. Cook, uncovered, for about 10 minutes, stirring occasionally and scraping up any browned bits from pan, until apple is soft and glazed. Spoon over pork chops. Serves 4.

1 serving: 273 Calories; 9.2 g Total Fat; 73 mg Sodium; 24 g Protein; 23 g Carbohydrate; 1 g Dietary Fibre

Pasta Spirals

Chunks of ham and pretty bits of pepper. Delicious, creamy and cheesy.

Fusilli pasta (about 8 oz., 225 g)	2 1/2 cups	625 mL
Boiling water	8 cups	2 L
Salt	2 tsp.	10 mL
Hard margarine (or butter)	1 tbsp.	15 mL
All-purpose flour	1 tbsp.	15 mL
Salt	1/2 tsp.	2 mL
Pepper	1/4 tsp.	1 mL
Milk	1 cup	250 mL
Chopped cooked ham (or chicken)	1 cup	250 mL
Green onions, chopped	3	3
Grated medium Cheddar cheese	1 cup	250 mL

Cook pasta in boiling water and salt in large uncovered pot or Dutch oven for 5 to 7 minutes until tender but firm. Drain. Return to pot. Cover. Keep warm.

While pasta is cooking, melt margarine in medium saucepan. Mix in flour, salt and pepper until smooth. Stir in milk until boiling and slightly thickened. Add to drained pasta. Stir.

Add ham, green onion and cheese. Stir. Makes 4 cups (1 L).

1 cup (250 mL): 451 Calories; 17.5 g Total Fat; 1025 mg Sodium; 24 g Protein; 48 g Carbohydrate; 2 g Dietary Fibre

Variation: Omit cooked ham. Use 6 1/2 oz. (184 g) can of flaked ham (or chicken), drained and broken up.

Hot Sausage And Bean Risotto

Very Italian with the subtle wine flavour. Perfect creamy consistency. Start sausages frying in pressure cooker, then chop onion and garlic.

Italian sausages (about 14 oz., 395 g), casings removed	3 – 4	3 – 4
Olive (or cooking) oil	1 tbsp.	15 mL
Finely chopped onion	2/3 cup	150 mL
Garlic cloves, minced (or 1/2 tsp., 2 mL, powder)	2	2
Hard margarine (or butter)	1 tbsp.	15 mL
Arborio rice	2 cups	500 mL
Dry white (or alcohol-free) wine	1/2 cup	125 mL
Prepared chicken broth	4 cups	1 L
Frozen whole green beans (about 4 oz., 113 g)	1 cup	250 mL
Freshly grated Parmesan cheese	1/2 cup	125 mL
Pepper	1/2 tsp.	2 mL

Fry sausages in olive oil in pressure cooker on medium for 7 to 9 minutes, turning occasionally, until browned. Cut into 3/4 inch (2 cm) thick slices. Set aside.

Sauté onion and garlic in margarine in same pressure cooker for about 3 minutes until onion is soft.

Add rice. Stir until well coated. Add wine. Heat and stir for 1 minute until liquid is absorbed.

Add broth. Stir. Lock lid in place. Bring pressure cooker up to pressure on high. Reduce heat to medium-low just to maintain even pressure. Cook for 8 minutes. Remove from heat. Allow pressure to drop naturally. Remove lid.

Add green beans and sausage. Stir. Cover, but do not lock lid in place. Let stand for 10 minutes until hot.

Add Parmesan cheese and pepper. Stir. Makes 8 cups (2 L).

1 cup (250 mL): 463 Calories; 21.9 g Total Fat; 918 mg Sodium; 16 g Protein; 46 g Carbohydrate; trace Dietary Fibre

Main Dishes

Tenderloin Of Pork

Nicely browned medallions of pork with citrusy "au jus."
Very tender with subtle lemon flavour.

Cooking oil	1 tbsp.	15 mL
Pork tenderloin, cut on diagonal into 1/2 inch (12 mm) slices	1 lb.	454 g
Lemon pepper, sprinkle		
Apple juice	1/3 cup	75 mL
Lemon juice	1 1/2 tbsp.	25 mL
Water	1 tbsp.	15 mL
Worcestershire sauce	1 tsp.	5 mL
Chopped fresh parsley (optional)	1 tbsp.	15 mL

Heat cooking oil in large frying pan on medium-high until hot. Add pork. Sprinkle with lemon pepper. Brown for about 2 minutes. Turn over. Sprinkle with lemon pepper. Brown for about 2 minutes. Transfer to plate. Keep warm.

Add next 4 ingredients to same frying pan. Heat and stir, scraping up any browned bits from pan, until simmering. Pour over pork.

Sprinkle parsley over pork. Serves 4.

1 serving: 208 Calories; 10.6 g Total Fat; 73 mg Sodium; 23 g Protein; 3 g Carbohydrate; trace Dietary Fibre

 To save time in recipes calling for both salt and pepper, keep a shaker filled with a ratio of 4 times as much salt as pepper, adjusting to suit your personal taste.

Pictured on page 125.

Glazed Ham Steak

This thick sauce forms a glaze around the ham steak,
adding a bit of sweetness. Quite pleasing.

Smoked ham steak, trimmed of fat	1 lb.	454 g
Brown sugar, packed	1/3 cup	75 mL
Apple cider vinegar	1 tbsp.	15 mL
Grainy mustard	2 tsp.	10 mL

Lightly brown ham on both sides in medium non-stick frying pan on medium-high. Reduce heat to medium.

While ham is browning, mix brown sugar, vinegar and mustard in small bowl. Spoon and spread 1/2 of brown sugar mixture over ham. Turn ham over. Spoon and spread remaining brown sugar mixture over ham. Simmer, uncovered, for 3 to 4 minutes turning often, until sauce is thickened. Serves 4.

1 serving: 214 Calories; 5 g Total Fat; 1487 mg Sodium; 22 g Protein; 19 g Carbohydrate; 0 g Dietary Fibre

SAUCY CANNED MEAT: Omit ham steak. Use 1 can (12 oz., 340 g) of processed meat (such as Prem or Spam). Slice. Follow steps above.

1. Salmon And Sun-Dried Tomato Pasta, page 102
2. Grilled Vegetable Salad, page 40
3. Tenderloin Of Pork, page 123

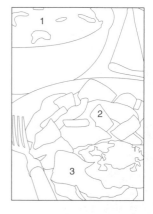

Main Dishes

Caramel Ice Cream Sauce

Serve this rich sauce warm over ice cream and sliced bananas. Yum!
Leftover sauce can be stored in the refrigerator for up to 3 weeks.

Hard margarine (or butter)	1/4 cup	60 mL
Granulated sugar	1/3 cup	75 mL
Brown sugar, packed	1 1/4 cups	300 mL
Salt	1/4 tsp.	1 mL
Evaporated milk	2/3 cup	150 mL
Vanilla	1 tsp.	5 mL

Melt margarine in medium saucepan. Add next 4 ingredients. Heat and stir on medium until boiling. Cook, without stirring, for 5 minutes.

Remove from heat. Stir in vanilla. Serve immediately. Sauce will separate as it sits. Stir well before serving to get consistency back. To re-warm, microwave in microwave-safe bowl on medium (50%), stirring every 30 seconds until heated through. Makes about 1 2/3 cups (400 mL).

2 tbsp. (30 mL): 151 Calories; 4.6 g Total Fat; 107 mg Sodium; 1 g Protein; 27 g Carbohydrate; 0 g Dietary Fibre

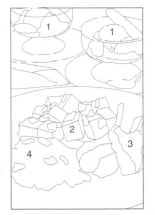

1. Pear Sauté Dessert, page 132
2. Sweet Potato With Basil, page 64
3. Coconut Grilled Lamb Chops, page 141
4. Beans With Onion, page 67

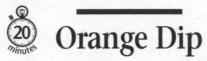

Orange Dip

Tangy orange flavour that's perfect for dipping bananas and other fresh fruits. Try spooned over canned fruit cocktail or fresh fruit salad.

Orange marmalade	2 tbsp.	30 mL
Light sour cream	1/2 cup	125 mL
Salt, sprinkle		

Microwave marmalade in small microwave-safe bowl on high (100%) for 15 seconds. Stir.

Add sour cream and salt. Mix well. Let stand for 15 minutes. Makes 3/4 cup (175 mL).

2 tbsp. (30 mL): 33 Calories; 1.4 g Total Fat; 12 mg Sodium; 1 g Protein; 5 g Carbohydrate; 0 g Dietary Fibre

Fruit Broil

Sweet pudding-like texture. First bite with the brown sugar is the best.

Can of plums (or apricots) in heavy syrup, drained	14 oz.	398 mL
Vanilla yogurt	2 cups	500 mL
Brown sugar, packed	1/4 cup	60 mL
Brown sugar, packed	6 tbsp.	100 mL

Cut plums in half. Remove and discard stones. Divide plums among 4 broiler-proof 4 oz. (114 mL) ramekins.

Stir yogurt and first amount of brown sugar in small bowl. Divide and spoon over plums.

Divide and sprinkle second amount of brown sugar over yogurt mixture. Broil about 8 inches (20 cm) from heat for about 4 minutes until sugar is dissolved. Serves 4.

1 serving: 295 Calories; 2.5 g Total Fat; 89 mg Sodium; 6 g Protein; 66 g Carbohydrate; 1 g Dietary Fibre

Sweet Chocolate Pie

Creamy, rich, melt-in-your-mouth chocolate flavour—chocolate crust, chocolate filling and chocolate curls on top!

Sweet chocolate baking squares (1 oz., 28 g, each), cut up	8	8
Block of cream cheese, softened	8 oz.	250 g
Icing (confectioner's) sugar	2/3 cup	150 mL
Frozen whipped topping, thawed	6 cups	1.5 L
Commercial chocolate wafer crumb crust (9 inch, 22 cm, size)	1	1
Chocolate curls, for garnish	1/2 cup	125 mL

Heat chocolate in heavy medium saucepan on lowest heat, stirring often, until just melted. Or microwave, uncovered, in medium microwave-safe bowl on medium-high (70%), stirring every 15 seconds, until just melted. Let stand at room temperature, stirring once or twice.

While chocolate is standing, beat cream cheese and icing sugar together in large bowl until smooth. Add chocolate. Beat well.

Fold in whipped topping. Turn into crust.

Garnish with chocolate curls. Chill. Cuts into 10 wedges.

1 wedge: 459 Calories; 30.9 g Total Fat; 188 mg Sodium; 4 g Protein; 46 g Carbohydrate; 0 g Dietary Fibre

Pictured on front cover.

Paré Pointer

If you put cocoa beans with a caribou, you might get a chocolate mousse.

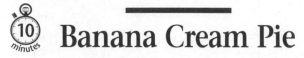

Banana Cream Pie

The perfect-tasting banana cream pie. Creamy and rich,
yet not overly sweet. Simple and delicious. Have frozen
whipped topping defrosting in the refrigerator during the day.

Instant vanilla pudding powder (6 serving size)	1	1
Milk	1 cup	250 mL
Medium bananas	2	2
Frozen whipped topping, thawed	1 cup	250 mL
Commercial 9 inch (22 cm) chocolate (or graham cracker crumb) crust	1	1
Frozen whipped topping, thawed	1 cup	250 mL
Banana chips, for garnish		

Beat pudding powder and milk together in medium bowl until smooth.

Slice bananas directly into pudding. Fold in first amount of topping. Turn into crust.

Spread second amount of topping over pudding mixture.

Garnish with banana chips. Cuts into 8 wedges.

1 wedge: 298 Calories; 13 g Total Fat; 376 mg Sodium; 3 g Protein; 44 g Carbohydrate; trace Dietary Fibre

Pictured on page 143.

 tip   *To use overripe bananas, cut into small slices. Put into small resealable freezer bag. Freeze. Add frozen to smoothies or use, thawed and mashed, in your favourite banana bread recipe.*

Plum Almond Crumble

Crumbles have always been a great comforting winter dessert. The addition of plums, coconut and almonds in this crumble makes it extra special.

Cans of plums in heavy syrup (14 oz., 398 mL, each), drained	2	2
Finely grated orange zest	1 tsp.	5 mL
All-purpose flour	1/2 cup	125 mL
Long thread coconut	1/3 cup	75 mL
Brown sugar, packed	6 tbsp.	100 mL
Sliced almonds	3 tbsp.	50 mL
Hard margarine (or butter), melted	1/4 cup	60 mL
Ground cloves	1/8 tsp.	0.5 mL

Cut plums in half. Remove and discard stones. Combine plums and orange zest in small bowl. Divide among 6 lightly greased ovenproof 4 oz. (114 mL) ramekins.

Combine remaining 6 ingredients in medium bowl. Divide and sprinkle over plum mixture. Bake in 375°F (190°C) oven for 15 to 20 minutes until golden. Serve warm. Serves 6.

1 serving: 308 Calories; 13.6 g Total Fat; 120 mg Sodium; 3 g Protein; 47 g Carbohydrate; 2 g Dietary Fibre

Pictured on page 144.

Variation: Can be made in lightly greased 1 quart (1 L) deep baking dish. Bake for about 20 minutes.

Paré Pointer
Fresh garden potatoes never see eye to eye.

Saucy Angel Food

Sweet and simple. Rich and creamy.

PECAN SAUCE

Brown sugar, packed	3/4 cup	175 mL
All-purpose flour	2 tbsp.	30 mL
Water	1 cup	250 mL
Chopped pecans	1/4 cup	60 mL
Commercial angel food cake, cut into 6 wedges	1	1

Pecan Sauce: Stir brown sugar and flour in small saucepan. Mix in water. Heat and stir until boiling and thickened.

Add pecans. Stir. Makes about 1 1/2 cups (375 mL) sauce.

Lay 1 cake wedge on each of 6 dessert plates. Spoon about 1/4 cup (60 mL) sauce over each wedge. Serves 6.

1 serving: 300 Calories; 4 g Total Fat; 436 mg Sodium; 4 g Protein; 64 g Carbohydrate; 1 g Dietary Fibre

Pear Sauté Dessert

Creamy, rich and sweet with a delicate hint of ginger.

Hard margarine (or butter)	2 tbsp.	30 mL
Brown sugar, packed	1/2 cup	125 mL
Ground cinnamon	1/4 tsp.	1 mL
Ground ginger	1/8 tsp.	0.5 mL
Ripe pears, peeled, cored and sliced	3	3
Vanilla ice cream	2 cups	500 mL
Crispy rolled store-bought cookies, for garnish		

Melt margarine in medium frying pan on medium. Stir in brown sugar, cinnamon and ginger. Heat and stir for about 1 minute until dark caramel colour.

(continued on next page)

Desserts

Add pears. Heat, stirring occasionally, until sauce is bubbling and pears are soft. Makes about 3 cups (750 mL) topping.

Divide and spoon ice cream into 4 small dessert bowls. Divide and spoon topping over ice cream.

Garnish with cookies. Serves 4.

1 serving: 335 Calories; 13.5 g Total Fat; 137 mg Sodium; 3 g Protein; 54 g Carbohydrate; 2 g Dietary Fibre

Pictured on page 126.

Grilled Pineapple Skewers

Brushing pineapple with Maple Rum Sauce while grilling enhances the pineapple's succulent sweetness. Serve with strawberry ice cream or frozen yogurt for a perfect summer dessert.

Bamboo skewers, 8 inch (20 cm) length	8	8
MAPLE RUM SAUCE		
Maple syrup	1/2 cup	125 mL
Spiced rum	1/4 cup	60 mL
Hard margarine (or butter)	1/4 cup	60 mL
Brown sugar, packed	1/4 cup	60 mL
Whole large pineapple (about 4 lbs., 1.8 kg)	1	1

Soak skewers in water for 10 minutes.

Maple Rum Sauce: Combine first 4 ingredients in medium saucepan. Heat and stir on medium for about 3 minutes until margarine is melted. Gently boil, without stirring, for 7 to 10 minutes until thickened. Makes about 3/4 cup (175 mL) sauce.

While skewers are soaking and sauce is cooking, peel pineapple. Cut into 1 inch (2.5 cm) chunks. Thread pineapple onto skewers. Brush with thickened sauce. Cook on greased grill over medium heat for about 15 minutes, turning and brushing occasionally with sauce, until lightly browned. Makes 8 skewers.

1 skewer: 211 Calories; 6.7 g Total Fat; 68 mg Sodium; 1 g Protein; 36 g Carbohydrate; 1 g Dietary Fibre

Pictured on page 144.

Steak Bunwiches

*Reserve a portion of the steak and beer mixture to get a head start
on Warm Steak Salad, page 135. Melted cheese helps hold the bun
and ingredients together, though it is still a bit messy.*

Beer (or alcohol-free beer)	1/2 cup	125 mL
Barbecue sauce	1/4 cup	60 mL
Grainy mustard	3 tbsp.	50 mL
Rib-eye steak (cut 1 inch, 2.5 cm, thick), trimmed of fat	2 1/2 lbs.	1.1 kg
Sliced onion	2 cups	500 mL
Cooking oil	1 tbsp.	15 mL
Hamburger buns, split	4	4
Mayonnaise (not salad dressing)	1/4 cup	60 mL
Grainy mustard	2 tbsp.	30 mL
Swiss cheese slices	4	4

Preheat barbecue to medium. While barbecue is heating, combine beer,
barbecue sauce and first amount of mustard in small bowl.

Cut steak into 6 equal pieces. Put 2 pieces of steak into shallow, non-reactive
dish or resealable freezer bag. Pour 1/3 cup (75 mL) beer mixture over steak.
Stir or turn to coat. Cover or seal. Marinate in refrigerator overnight. Use in
Warm Steak Salad, page 135. Cook remaining steak pieces on greased grill for
5 to 7 minutes per side, basting several times with beer mixture, until desired
doneness. Let stand for 5 minutes. Slice thinly across grain. Keep warm.

While steak is cooking, sauté onion in cooking oil in large frying pan for about
10 minutes until lightly browned.

While onion is sautéing, arrange bun halves, cut side down, on greased grill.
Toast for about 2 minutes until lightly browned. Keep warm.

Combine mayonnaise and second amount of mustard in small bowl. Spread
on cut side of each bun half.

Divide and layer steak, onion and cheese on bottom halves of buns. Top with
top halves of buns. Makes 4 bunwiches.

*1 bunwich: 671 Calories; 35.6 g Total Fat; 771 mg Sodium; 52 g Protein; 33 g Carbohydrate;
2 g Dietary Fibre*

Warm Steak Salad

Uses part of steak and beer mixture from Steak Bunwiches, page 134.
A very attractive salad. Blue cheese and beef are a perfect combination.
Serve with crusty bread.

Reserved portion of steak in beer marinade, page 134	2	2
BALSAMIC DRESSING		
Olive (or cooking) oil	1/4 cup	60 mL
Balsamic vinegar	3 tbsp.	50 mL
Liquid honey	1 tbsp.	15 mL
Garlic clove, minced (or 1/4 tsp., 1 mL, powder)	1	1
Small ripe pears, with skin	2	2
Bag of mixed salad greens (about 4 cups, 1 L)	4 1/2 oz.	128 g
Crumbled blue cheese (about 2 oz., 57 g)	1/2 cup	125 mL
Chopped walnuts	1/2 cup	125 mL

Preheat barbecue to medium. While barbecue is heating, remove reserved steak from marinade. Reserve beer mixture for basting. Cook steak on greased grill over medium heat for 5 to 7 minutes per side, basting several times with beer mixture, until desired doneness. Discard any remaining beer mixture. Let steak stand for 5 minutes. Thinly slice across grain. Keep warm.

Balsamic Dressing: While steak is cooking, combine next 4 ingredients in jar with tight-fitting lid. Shake well. Makes 1/2 cup (125 mL) dressing.

While steak is standing, remove stem end and core from pears. Slice thinly. Put salad greens into large bowl. Add pear, blue cheese and walnuts. Drizzle dressing over salad. Add steak. Toss. Makes 7 cups (1.75 L). Serves 4 to 6.

1 serving: 526 Calories; 36 g Total Fat; 419 mg Sodium; 30 g Protein; 23 g Carbohydrate; 4 g Dietary Fibre

Herb And Cheese Burgers

Reserve some of Patty Mixture for use in Creamy Tomato Meatballs,
page 137. Serve these burgers with sliced grilled pineapple,
spinach leaves, fried onion and mayonnaise.

PATTY MIXTURE

Lean ground beef	2 lbs.	900 g
Grated sharp Cheddar cheese	1 cup	250 mL
Large eggs, fork-beaten	2	2
Fine dry bread crumbs	1 cup	250 mL
Finely chopped onion	2/3 cup	150 mL
Garlic cloves, minced (or 1 tsp., 5 mL, powder)	4	4
Chopped fresh sweet basil (or 4 tsp., 20 mL, dried)	1/3 cup	75 mL
Chopped fresh parsley (or 4 tsp., 20 mL, flakes)	1/3 cup	75 mL
Salt	1/2 tsp.	2 mL
Pepper	1/2 tsp.	2 mL
Ground cumin	1 tbsp.	15 mL
Hamburger buns, split	6	6

Patty Mixture: Preheat barbecue to medium. While barbecue is heating, combine first 11 ingredients in large bowl. Mix well. Divide and shape 1/2 of mixture into 6 patties about 5 inches (12.5 cm) in diameter. Cover and chill remaining ground beef mixture (about 2 3/4 cups, 675 mL) for use in Creamy Tomato Meatballs, page 137. Cook patties on greased grill over medium heat for about 6 minutes per side until no longer pink inside.

While patties are cooking, arrange bun halves, cut side down, on grill. Toast for about 2 minutes until lightly browned. Place patties on bottom halves of buns. Layer with your choice of toppings. Place top halves of buns over patties. Makes 6 burgers.

1 burger: 337 Calories; 13.5 g Total Fat; 535 mg Sodium; 22 g Protein; 30 g Carbohydrate;
1 g Dietary Fibre

Creamy Tomato Meatballs

Uses part of ground beef mixture from Herb And Cheese Burgers, page 136.
Serve these saucy meatballs over hot pasta with a green salad,
steamed beans or asparagus, and garlic toast.

Reserved portion of Patty Mixture, page 136	2 3/4 cups	675 mL
Cooking oil	1 tbsp.	15 mL
Chopped onion	1 cup	250 mL
Garlic cloves, minced (or 1/2 tsp., 2 mL, powder)	2	2
Bacon slices, diced	4	4
Cooking oil	1 tbsp.	15 mL
Can of diced tomatoes, with juice	19 oz.	540 mL
Whipping (or half-and-half) cream	1 cup	250 mL
Salt	1/4 tsp.	1 mL
Pepper	1/4 tsp.	1 mL

Divide and shape reserved Patty Mixture into 12 meatballs.

Cook meatballs in first amount of cooking oil in large frying pan on medium for about 15 minutes, turning occasionally, until no longer pink inside. Remove to paper towel to drain.

Meanwhile, sauté onion, garlic and bacon in second amount of cooking oil in large saucepan for about 10 minutes until onion is soft and bacon is browned. Transfer to food processor.

Add remaining 4 ingredients to bacon mixture. Process until smooth. Return mixture to same large saucepan. Heat and stir on medium for about 5 minutes until hot. Add meatballs. Stir until meatballs are well coated. Serves 4.

1 serving: 718 Calories; 54.3 g Total Fat; 963 mg Sodium; 34 g Protein; 25 g Carbohydrate; 3 g Dietary Fibre

Paré Pointer
A banana doctor is needed when a banana isn't peeling well.

Lemon Chicken Pasta

Reserve some of the chicken mixture for Chicken Asparagus Frittata, page 139.
Beautiful herbed pasta. Sauce coats every item, making this dish very flavourful.

LEMON GARLIC CHICKEN

Boneless, skinless chicken breast halves (about 8), cubed	2 lbs.	900 g
Garlic cloves, minced (or 1 1/2 tsp., 7 mL, powder)	6	6
Chopped fresh parsley (or 2 tbsp., 30 mL, flakes)	1/2 cup	125 mL
Olive (or cooking) oil	1/4 cup	60 mL
Grainy mustard	2 tbsp.	30 mL
Finely grated lemon zest	2 tbsp.	30 mL
Freshly squeezed lemon juice	1/4 cup	60 mL
Pepper	1 tsp.	5 mL
Chopped fresh rosemary leaves (or 1/2 tsp., 2 mL, dried)	2 tsp.	10 mL
Penne pasta (about 1 lb., 454 g)	2 1/2 cups	625 mL
Boiling water	8 cups	2 L
Salt	1/4 tsp.	1 mL
Finely grated Parmesan cheese	1/2 cup	125 mL

Lemon Garlic Chicken: Combine first 9 ingredients in large bowl. Mix well. Divide mixture in half. Cover and chill 1 portion for Chicken Asparagus Frittata, page 139. Stir-fry remaining portion in large frying pan on medium-high for about 10 minutes until chicken is no longer pink.

Meanwhile, cook pasta in boiling water and salt in large uncovered pot or Dutch oven for 10 to 12 minutes, stirring occasionally, until tender but firm. Drain.

Combine chicken mixture, pasta and Parmesan cheese in large serving bowl. Makes about 8 cups (2 L).

1 cup (250 mL): 233 Calories; 7 g Total Fat; 153 mg Sodium; 19 g Protein; 22 g Carbohydrate; 1 g Dietary Fibre

Chicken Asparagus Frittata

Uses a portion of the chicken mixture from Lemon Chicken Pasta,
page 138. Fabulous taste. Hint of lemon and rosemary.
Very Mediterranean. Serve with Caesar salad and crusty rolls.

Reserved portion of Lemon Garlic Chicken, page 138	2 1/2 cups	625 mL
Finely chopped fresh asparagus	1 cup	250 mL
Large eggs, fork-beaten	8	8
All-purpose flour	1/4 cup	60 mL
Salt	1/2 tsp.	2 mL
Finely grated Parmesan cheese	1/2 cup	125 mL

Combine first 5 ingredients in large bowl. Turn mixture into greased, parchment paper-lined 9 x 13 inch (22 x 33 cm) pan.

Sprinkle Parmesan cheese over chicken mixture. Bake in 350°F (175°C) oven for about 30 minutes until set. Let stand for 5 minutes. Serve warm or cold. Cuts into 8 pieces.

1 piece: 224 Calories; 11.6 g Total Fat; 394 mg Sodium; 23 g Protein; 6 g Carbohydrate;
1 g Dietary Fibre

To avoid an unexpected trip to the grocery store while making dinner, keep staple ingredients on hand, such as pasta, rice, frozen vegetables, fresh vegetables that last (such as onions, carrots, peppers and potatoes), frozen meats, canned and boxed soups, basic seasonings (such as salt, pepper, garlic powder, garlic salt, seasoning salt, dried oregano, dried sweet basil and cayenne pepper), and sauces (such as barbecue, soy, teriyaki and Worcestershire).

Spicy Moroccan Chicken

Prepare and marinate ahead of time and just throw it in the oven when you get home. Attractive combination of colours and textures. The aroma while this is cooking is fabulous—and so is its taste. An adventure in spices!

White (or alcohol-free) wine	1/2 cup	125 mL
Liquid honey	3 tbsp.	50 mL
Olive (or cooking) oil	1 tbsp.	15 mL
Ground cumin	2 tsp.	10 mL
Ground coriander	2 tsp.	10 mL
Chili powder	1 tsp.	5 mL
Ground cinnamon	1/2 tsp.	2 mL
Medium onion, sliced	1	1
Garlic cloves, minced (or 1 tsp., 5 mL, powder)	4	4
Pitted prunes	2/3 cup	150 mL
Dried apricots, halved	2/3 cup	150 mL
Salt	1/2 tsp.	2 mL
Pepper	1/2 tsp.	2 mL
Boneless, skinless chicken thighs, halved	2 lbs.	900 g

In the morning (or the night before), combine first 13 ingredients in ungreased 2 quart (2 L) shallow casserole.

Add chicken. Turn to coat. Cover. Chill for at least 8 hours or overnight. Stir. Bake chicken, uncovered, in 400°F (205°C) oven for about 30 minutes, stirring occasionally, until chicken is no longer pink. Serves 8.

1 serving: 255 Calories; 6.6 g Total Fat; 156 mg Sodium; 23 g Protein; 25 g Carbohydrate; 2 g Dietary Fibre

 Freeze meat and marinades together in resealable freezer bags. After the meat is thawed, you are ready to cook. This method uses less marinade, so this is a money saving tip too!

Coconut Grilled Lamb Chops

Marinate these chops a day ahead and they are all ready to grill for dinner the next day. Juicy, succulent and tender.

MARINADE		
Light coconut milk	1/2 cup	125 mL
Satay sauce	1/3 cup	75 mL
Oyster sauce	1/4 cup	60 mL
Lime juice	1/4 cup	60 mL
Sweet chili sauce	2 tbsp.	30 mL
Brown sugar, packed	2 tbsp.	30 mL
Finely grated gingerroot (or 1/2 tsp., 2 mL, ground ginger)	2 tsp.	10 mL
Garlic cloves, minced (or 1/2 tsp., 2 mL, powder)	2	2
Rack of lamb (8 ribs), trimmed of fat	1 lb.	454 g
SATAY SAUCE		
Satay sauce	1/3 cup	75 mL
Water	3 tbsp.	50 mL
Chopped fresh cilantro	3 tbsp.	50 mL

Marinade: Combine first 8 ingredients in large bowl.

Separate rack of lamb into chops by slicing between rib bones. Add to marinade. Stir to coat. Cover. Chill for at least 3 hours or overnight.

Preheat barbecue to medium-high. While barbecue is heating, remove lamb chops from marinade. Discard marinade. Cook chops on greased grill for 5 to 7 minutes per side until desired doneness.

Satay Sauce: While chops are cooking, combine all 3 ingredients in medium saucepan. Heat and stir on medium-low for about 3 minutes until hot. Makes about 1/2 cup (125 mL) sauce. Drizzle over chops. Serves 4.

1 serving: 256 Calories; 16.6 g Total Fat; 1354 mg Sodium; 16 g Protein; 13 g Carbohydrate; 1 g Dietary Fibre

Pictured on page 126.

Pineapple Steak

Pineapple juice in the marinade tenderizes as well as flavours the steak. Tender, moist and juicy. Could be served with a grilled pineapple ring as an accompaniment or with Salad Mix, page 43, and Beans With Onion, page 67.

MARINADE		
Pineapple juice	2 cups	500 mL
White (or alcohol-free) wine	1/2 cup	125 mL
Soy sauce	1/3 cup	75 mL
Apple cider vinegar	1/4 cup	60 mL
Onion powder	1/4 tsp.	1 mL
Round steak (3/4 inch, 2 cm, thick), cut into 10 serving-size pieces	2 1/2 lbs.	1.1 kg

Marinade: Combine first 5 ingredients in large bowl.

Place steak in shallow non-reactive dish or resealable freezer bag. Pour marinade over steak. Stir or turn to coat. Cover or seal. Let stand for at least 8 hours or overnight.

Preheat barbecue to high. While barbecue is heating, remove steak from marinade. Discard marinade. Sear steak on both sides on greased grill. Cook for about 5 minutes per side until desired doneness. Serves 10.

1 serving: 160 Calories; 4.3 g Total Fat; 328 mg Sodium; 24 g Protein; 4 g Carbohydrate; trace Dietary Fibre

1. Quick Lemon Squares, page 148
2. Banana Cream Pie, page 130

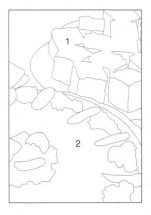

Barley Beef Soup

This slow-cooker soup is a thick and hearty meal in itself!
You'll need about 15 minutes to prepare the ingredients before you
leave for work—but no time at all when you get home! Just pile some
Crusty Cheese Biscuits, page 38, in a basket and you're set.

Extra lean ground beef	1/2 lb.	225 g
Large onion, chopped	1	1
Olive (or cooking) oil	1 tbsp.	15 mL
Package of shredded coleslaw mix (about 8 1/2 cups, 2.1 L)	16 oz.	454 g
Can of diced tomatoes, with juice	14 oz.	398 mL
Frozen mixed vegetables	1 cup	250 mL
Can of condensed beef broth	10 oz.	284 mL
Water	6 cups	1.5 L
Pearl barley	1/2 cup	125 mL
Bay leaf	1	1
Dried whole oregano	1 tsp.	5 mL
Beef bouillon powder	1 tbsp.	15 mL

Scramble-fry ground beef and onion in olive oil in medium frying pan on medium-high until onion is soft and beef is no longer pink. Turn into 5 to 6 quart (5 to 6 L) slow cooker.

Add remaining 9 ingredients. Stir well. Cover. Cook on Low for 6 to 7 hours or on High for 3 to 3 1/2 hours until barley and vegetables are tender. Makes about 12 1/2 cups (3.1 L).

1 cup (250 mL): 119 Calories; 4.1 g Total Fat; 375 mg Sodium; 8 g Protein; 13 g Carbohydrate; 2 g Dietary Fibre

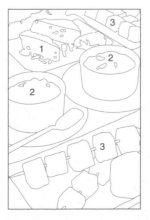

1. Fudge Sauced Brownies, page 149
2. Plum Almond Crumble, page 131
3. Grilled Pineapple Skewers, page 133

Sausage Chowder

Spicy, chunky slow-cooker soup with a mild mustard flavour.
Spinach and carrot add great colour—no garnish needed. Takes only
10 minutes in the morning to prepare and about 20 minutes
to finish before serving.

Medium onion, chopped	1	1
Spicy sausages, sliced into 1/2 inch (12 mm) coins	12 oz.	340 g
Bags of frozen California vegetable mix (1 lb., 454 g, each)	2	2
Can of condensed chicken broth	10 oz.	284 mL
Can of evaporated milk	5 1/2 oz.	160 mL
Prepared mustard	1 tbsp.	15 mL
Pepper	1/4 tsp.	1 mL
Water	5 cups	1.25 L
Instant potato flakes	1 1/2 cups	375 mL
Fresh spinach leaves, cut chiffonade (see Note)	2 cups	500 mL

Fry onion and sausage in large non-stick frying pan for 4 to 5 minutes until onion is soft and sausage is lightly browned. Turn into 3 1/2 quart (3.5 L) slow cooker.

Add next 6 ingredients. Cover. Cook on Low for 7 to 8 hours or on High for 3 1/2 to 4 hours.

Slowly add potato flakes, stirring constantly. Add spinach. Cover. Cook on High for about 15 minutes until soup is slightly thickened. Makes 11 1/2 cups (2.9 L).

1 cup (250 mL): 184 Calories; 11 g Total Fat; 451 mg Sodium; 9 g Protein; 13 g Carbohydrate; 2 g Dietary Fibre

Note: To cut chiffonade, simply stack a few leaves at a time and roll up tightly. Slice crosswise into very thin strips.

Turkey With Apricot Sauce

Turkey is moist and juicy; sauce is delicate and sweet.

Boneless, skinless turkey breast	1 1/2 lbs.	680 g
APRICOT SAUCE		
Apricot jam	1/2 cup	125 mL
White vinegar	2 tsp.	10 mL
Soy sauce	1 tsp.	5 mL
Ground ginger	1/4 tsp.	1 mL
Paprika	1/4 tsp.	1 mL
Water	2 tbsp.	30 mL
Cornstarch	1 tbsp.	15 mL

Place turkey breast in oblong 4 quart (4 L) slow cooker. Cut in half if too large to fit.

Apricot Sauce: Mix first 5 ingredients in small bowl. Spread on turkey. Cover. Cook on Low for 3 1/2 to 4 hours or on High for 2 to 2 1/2 hours until meat is tender and no longer pink. Remove turkey to serving platter. Keep warm. Transfer liquid to small saucepan.

Stir water into cornstarch in small bowl until smooth. Stir into liquid until boiling and thickened. Makes about 1 1/4 cups (300 mL) sauce. Serves 6.

1 serving: 200 Calories; 0.8 g Total Fat; 125 mg Sodium; 28 g Protein; 20 g Carbohydrate; trace Dietary Fibre

Paré Pointer

Baby fish like to swim into a concrete wall so they can say "dam" without their parents scolding them.

Quick Lemon Squares

Make these tangy squares the day before to allow crackers to soften.
Tangy lemon flavour. Pretty layered look. No baking.

Whole graham crackers	36	36
FILLING		
Can of sweetened condensed milk	11 oz.	300 mL
Freshly squeezed lemon juice	2/3 cup	150 mL
LEMON GLAZE		
Freshly squeezed lemon juice	2 tbsp.	30 mL
Icing (confectioner's) sugar	1 cup	250 mL
Milk (or semi-sweet) chocolate chips	1 tbsp.	15 mL

Lightly dampen 8 × 8 inch (20 × 20 cm) pan with water to hold waxed paper in place. Line with waxed or parchment paper, cut to fit. Fit 9 graham crackers on bottom of pan.

Filling: Stir condensed milk and lemon juice together in small bowl until thick and smooth. Makes 1 2/3 cups (400 mL) filling. Spoon generous 1/2 cup (125 mL) filling over graham crackers. Spread evenly. Repeat with remaining crackers and filling, beginning and ending with cracker layers.

Lemon Glaze: Slowly stir lemon juice, 1 tsp. (5 mL) at a time, into icing sugar in small dish until a barely pourable consistency. Carefully spread over top cracker layer.

Put chocolate chips into 1 corner of small resealable freezer bag. Press air out and seal. Immerse corner of bag in small cup of hot water for about 3 minutes. Mash chocolate chips until smooth using fingers. Immerse in hot water again if necessary until chocolate is completely melted. Push melted chocolate down into 1 corner of bag. Snip off small piece of corner. Squeeze chocolate in thin zigzags over glaze. Cover. Chill for at least 10 hours or overnight until crackers are softened. Cuts into 36 squares.

1 square: 81 Calories; 1.7 g Total Fat; 56 mg Sodium; 1 g Protein; 15 g Carbohydrate; trace Dietary Fibre

Pictured on page 143.

Fudge Sauced Brownies

Rich chocolate flavour and a hint of flavour
from the pecans. The sauce is smooth and dark.

Butter (not margarine), chopped	9 oz.	255 g
Semi-sweet chocolate baking squares (1 oz., 28 g, each), chopped	8	8
Granulated sugar	2 1/4 cups	550 mL
Large eggs, fork-beaten	5	5
Pecans, chopped	3/4 cup	175 mL
All-purpose flour	1 cup	250 mL
Baking powder	1/2 tsp.	2 mL
Cocoa, sifted if lumpy	1/2 cup	125 mL
FUDGE SAUCE		
Whipping cream	3/4 cup	175 mL
Semi-sweet chocolate baking squares (1 oz., 28 g, each), chopped	8	8
Large marshmallows, chopped	12	12

Combine butter and chocolate in large microwave-safe bowl. Microwave, uncovered, on high (100%) for about 2 minutes, stirring twice during cooking, until melted. Cool.

Add sugar, eggs and pecans. Mix well.

Add flour, baking powder and cocoa. Mix well. Pour chocolate mixture into greased 8 x 12 inch (20 x 30 cm) microwave-safe dish. Microwave, uncovered, on medium (50%) for about 15 minutes, turning dish at halftime if microwave doesn't have turntable, until almost set in middle. Cool. Cover. Chill for at least 8 hours or overnight. Cut into 28 triangles.

Fudge Sauce: Combine whipping cream, chocolate and marshmallows in medium microwave-safe dish. Microwave, uncovered, on high (100%) for 1 minute. Stir. Microwave, uncovered, on medium (50%) for 1 to 2 minutes until marshmallows are melted. Stir. Makes about 1 2/3 cups (400 mL) sauce. Drizzle over brownies. Serves 14.

1 serving: 589 Calories; 35.6 g Total Fat; 199 mg Sodium; 6 g Protein; 70 g Carbohydrate; 4 g Dietary Fibre

Pictured on page 144.

Measurement Tables

Throughout this book measurements are given in Conventional and Metric measure. To compensate for differences between the two measurements due to rounding, a full metric measure is not always used. The cup used is the standard 8 fluid ounce. Temperature is given in degrees Fahrenheit and Celsius. Baking pan measurements are in inches and centimetres as well as quarts and litres. An exact metric conversion is given below as well as the working equivalent (Metric Standard Measure).

Spoons

Conventional Measure	Metric Exact Conversion Millilitre (mL)	Metric Standard Measure Millilitre (mL)
1/8 teaspoon (tsp.)	0.6 mL	0.5 mL
1/4 teaspoon (tsp.)	1.2 mL	1 mL
1/2 teaspoon (tsp.)	2.4 mL	2 mL
1 teaspoon (tsp.)	4.7 mL	5 mL
2 teaspoons (tsp.)	9.4 mL	10 mL
1 tablespoon (tbsp.)	14.2 mL	15 mL

Cups

Conventional Measure	Metric Exact Conversion Millilitre (mL)	Metric Standard Measure Millilitre (mL)
1/4 cup (4 tbsp.)	56.8 mL	60 mL
1/3 cup (5 1/3 tbsp.)	75.6 mL	75 mL
1/2 cup (8 tbsp.)	113.7 mL	125 mL
2/3 cup (10 2/3 tbsp.)	151.2 mL	150 mL
3/4 cup (12 tbsp.)	170.5 mL	175 mL
1 cup (16 tbsp.)	227.3 mL	250 mL
4 1/2 cups	1022.9 mL	1000 mL (1 L)

Oven Temperatures

Fahrenheit (°F)	Celsius (°C)
175°	80°
200°	95°
225°	110°
250°	120°
275°	140°
300°	150°
325°	160°
350°	175°
375°	190°
400°	205°
425°	220°
450°	230°
475°	240°
500°	260°

Dry Measurements

Conventional Measure Ounces (oz.)	Metric Exact Conversion Grams (g)	Metric Standard Measure Grams (g)
1 oz.	28.3 g	28 g
2 oz.	56.7 g	57 g
3 oz.	85.0 g	85 g
4 oz.	113.4 g	125 g
5 oz.	141.7 g	140 g
6 oz.	170.1 g	170 g
7 oz.	198.4 g	200 g
8 oz.	226.8 g	250 g
16 oz.	453.6 g	500 g
32 oz.	907.2 g	1000 g (1 kg)

Pans

Conventional Inches	Metric Centimetres
8x8 inch	20x20 cm
9x9 inch	22x22 cm
9x13 inch	22x33 cm
10x15 inch	25x38 cm
11x17 inch	28x43 cm
8x2 inch round	20x5 cm
9x2 inch round	22x5 cm
10x4 1/2 inch tube	25x11 cm
8x4x3 inch loaf	20x10x7.5 cm
9x5x3 inch loaf	22x12.5x7.5 cm

Casseroles

CANADA & BRITAIN Standard Size Casserole	Exact Metric Measure	UNITED STATES Standard Size Casserole	Exact Metric Measure
1 qt. (5 cups)	1.13 L	1 qt. (4 cups)	900 mL
1 1/2 qts. (7 1/2 cups)	1.69 L	1 1/2 qts. (6 cups)	1.35 L
2 qts. (10 cups)	2.25 L	2 qts. (8 cups)	1.8 L
2 1/2 qts. (12 1/2 cups)	2.81 L	2 1/2 qts. (10 cups)	2.25 L
3 qts. (15 cups)	3.38 L	3 qts. (12 cups)	2.7 L
4 qts. (20 cups)	4.5 L	4 qts. (16 cups)	3.6 L
5 qts. (25 cups)	5.63 L	5 qts. (20 cups)	4.5 L

Tip Index

Recipe Index

152

153

155

156

Company's Coming cookbooks are available at retail locations throughout Canada!

EXCLUSIVE mail order offer on next page

Buy any 2 cookbooks—choose a 3rd FREE of equal or less value than the lowest price paid.

Original Series   CA$14.99 Canada   US$10.99 USA & International

CODE		CODE		CODE	
SQ	150 Delicious Squares	KC	Kids Cooking	FD	Fondues
CA	Casseroles	CT	Cooking For Two	CCBE	The Beef Book
MU	Muffins & More	BB	Breakfasts & Brunches	ASI	Asian Cooking
SA	Salads	SC	Slow Cooker Recipes	CB	The Cheese Book
AP	Appetizers	ODM	One-Dish Meals	RC	The Rookie Cook
DE	Desserts	ST	Starters	RHR	Rush-Hour Recipes
SS	Soups & Sandwiches	SF	Stir-Fry	SW	Sweet Cravings
CO	Cookies	MAM	Make-Ahead Meals		
PA	Pasta	PB	The Potato Book		
BA	Barbecues	CCLFC	Low-Fat Cooking		
LR	Light Recipes	CCLFP	Low-Fat Pasta		
PR	Preserves	CFK	Cook For Kids		
CH	Chicken Etc.	SCH	Stews, Chilies & Chowders		

Greatest Hits Series

CODE	CA$12.99 Canada US$9.99 USA & International
ITAL	Italian
MEX	Mexican

Lifestyle Series

CODE	CA$16.99 Canada US$12.99 USA & International
GR	Grilling
DC	Diabetic Cooking

Special Occasion Series

CODE	CA$19.99 Canada US$17.99 USA & International
CE	Chocolate Everything
GFK	Gifts from the Kitchen
CFS	Cooking for the Seasons

Company's Coming

COOKBOOKS

COMPANY'S COMING PUBLISHING LIMITED
2311 - 96 Street
Edmonton, Alberta, Canada T6N 1G3
Tel: (780) 450-6223 Fax: (780) 450-1857
www.companyscoming.com

EXCLUSIVE Mail Order Offer

See previous page for list of cookbooks

Buy 2 Get 1 FREE!

Buy any 2 cookbooks—choose a **3rd FREE**
of equal or less value than the lowest price paid.

Quantity	Code	Title	Price Each	Price Total
			$	$
		DON'T FORGET		
		to indicate your		
		FREE BOOK(S).		
		(see exclusive mail order		
		offer above)		
		please print		
	TOTAL BOOKS (including FREE)	TOTAL BOOKS PURCHASED:	$	

	International	Canada & USA
Plus Shipping & Handling (per destination)	$7.00 (one book)	$5.00 (1-3 books)
Additional Books (including FREE books)	$ ($2.00 each)	$ ($1.00 each)
Sub-Total	$	$
Canadian residents add G.S.T.(7%)		$
TOTAL AMOUNT ENCLOSED	$	$

The Fine Print

- Orders outside Canada must be **PAID IN US FUNDS** by cheque or money order drawn on Canadian or US bank or by credit card.
- Make cheque or money order payable to: **COMPANY'S COMING PUBLISHING LIMITED.**
- Prices are expressed in Canadian dollars for Canada, US dollars for USA & International and are subject to change without prior notice.
- Orders are shipped surface mail. For courier rates, visit our web-site: **companyscoming.com** or contact us:
  Tel: (780) 450-6223 Fax: (780) 450-1857.
- Sorry, no C.O.D.'s.

Gift Giving

- Let us help you with your gift giving!
- We will send cookbooks directly to the recipients of your choice if you give us their names and addresses.
- Please specify the titles you wish to send to each person.
- If you would like to include your personal note or card, we will be pleased to enclose it with your gift order.
- Company's Coming Cookbooks make excellent gifts: Birthdays, bridal showers, Mother's Day, Father's Day, graduation or any occasion ...collect them all!

☐ MasterCard ☐ VISA

_____
Expiry date

Account # _____

Name of cardholder _____

Cardholder's signature _____

Shipping Address

Send the cookbooks listed above to:

Name: _____

Street: _____

City: _____ Prov./State: _____

Country: _____ Postal Code/Zip: _____

Tel: (___) _____

E-mail address: _____

☐ YES! Please send a catalogue

Special Occasion Series

Let *Home for the Holidays* help make this holiday season a memorable one with more than 190 all-new easy-to-follow recipes. It's your complete guide to holiday entertaining.

- Tree-Trimming Party
- Christmas is for Kids
- Gifts for the Host
- Know Your Turkey
- Christmas Goodies
- Boxing Day
- International Buffet
- Table Decorations
- Recipes—Appetizers to Desserts

Quick
&
Easy
Recipes

Everyday
Ingredients

Canada's
**most popular
cookbooks!**

Complete your Original Series Collection!

- ☐ 150 Delicious Squares
- ☐ Casseroles
- ☐ Muffins & More
- ☐ Salads
- ☐ Appetizers
- ☐ Desserts
- ☐ Soups & Sandwiches
- ☐ Cookies
- ☐ Pasta
- ☐ Barbecues
- ☐ Light Recipes
- ☐ Preserves
- ☐ Chicken Etc.
- ☐ Kids Cooking
- ☐ Cooking For Two
- ☐ Breakfasts & Brunches
- ☐ Slow Cooker Recipes
- ☐ One-Dish Meals
- ☐ Starters
- ☐ Stir-Fry
- ☐ Make-Ahead Meals
- ☐ The Potato Book
- ☐ Low-Fat Cooking
- ☐ Low-Fat Pasta
- ☐ Cook For Kids
- ☐ Stews, Chilies & Chowders
- ☐ Fondues
- ☐ The Beef Book
- ☐ Asian Cooking
- ☐ The Cheese Book
- ☐ The Rookie Cook
- ☐ Rush-Hour Recipes
- ☐ Sweet Cravings **NEW** Nov. 1/02

COLLECT ALL Company's Coming Series Cookbooks!

Greatest Hits Series
- ☐ Italian
- ☐ Mexican

Lifestyle Series
- ☐ Grilling
- ☐ Diabetic Cooking

Special Occasion Series
- ☐ Chocolate Everything
- ☐ Gifts from the Kitchen
- ☐ Cooking for the Seasons
- ☐ Home for the Holidays **NEW** Oct. 1/02

Canada's most popular cookbooks!